MOTOR
Trials and Tribulations

Arrol-Johnston 18hp of 1906 photographed in Pollok Park

MOTOR
Trials and Tribulations

GEORGE OLIVER

EDINBURGH : HMSO

British Library Cataloguing in Publication Data

A catalogue record for this book is available from the British Library

Front cover picture

The front cover of the Arrol-Johnston Catalogue

ISBN 0 11 495171 3

FOREWORD

To write this brief foreword to my great friend George Oliver's account of the Scottish motor vehicle industry gives me great pleasure, but sadness too; pleasure that the book is being published and sadness that its author did not live to see it in print.

George was not only a hugely respected historian with an unparalleled knowledge of the subject of this book; he was also a practical motorist with a lifelong enthusiasm for veteran and vintage motor cars of quality.

I wish for his book the success that it deserves.

Thomas Love
President: Veteran Car Club of Great Britain 1991-3

DIRECTOR'S PREFACE

The rise and fall of the Scottish motor vehicle manufacturing industry was a lifetime interest of the late George Oliver. He wrote with vigour and knowledge about the makers, the machines, the workshops and the factories and he accumulated an amazing collection of written material and photographs. Many of these photographs will appear for the first time in print in this book.

Glasgow Museums is indebted to his widow Cordelia for her generous gift of his archive to the Museum of Transport. We are also grateful for her help and encouragement with the book which will make a vital contribution to our knowledge of Scottish history.

Julian Spalding
Director, Glasgow Museums

Contents

Introduction

Until now the Scottish motor industry has not been adequately documented. Since the late 40s, almost without exception, its history has been misrepresented, with errors of fact occurring again and again, simply because it is so easy to copy what someone else has already said. This book is an attempt to put the record straight, as far as is possible.

I grew up in Glasgow during the 30s, when the screech of the clutch on Galbraith's chain-driven Albions was still an everyday sound and one was conscious always of the number of Albion commercial vehicles and buses in regular use. Apart from the local taxi, which was a rather tired 15/30 Argyll, I have no recollection of other Scottish makes, apart from the Halley which I remember when it was still in use. I knew it later, at the end of the 30s, when it was to be found at fairgrounds, generating current for roundabouts, or on the road, towing a caravan. Halleys, in fact, were engaged on the same kind of work until well after the Second World War.

Throughout the 50s I had the run of the Sword Collection of old cars. There were many of Scottish manufacture, from Arrol-Johnston dogcarts of the earliest years of the century to a 1928 single-sleeve Argyll, along with Beardmores (John Sword had no fewer than three examples), many Albions and a solitary Galloway. In time most of these cars passed into public ownership at the Glasgow Museum of Transport, thanks largely to the foresight of its Curator at the time, A S E Browning, and it is there that the largest and best collection of Scottish cars in the world is to be found.

George Oliver

Chapter One

Importers and Early Manufacturers 1895 - 1900

Albion A2 8hp dogcart with N O Fulton at the controls and Dr T Blackwood-Murray as a passenger

A Glasgow man, George Johnston, a consulting engineer who had been working on designs for self-propelled vehicles since 1895 (perhaps even earlier) began to build them commercially in 1900. This however, did not make him the first Scottish car manufacturer, that distinction goes to John Stirling of Hamilton, who had offered his car, the Stirling, from quite early in 1897.

In Glasgow, by the beginning of 1900 if not earlier, Alex Govan had begun to assemble Argyll voiturettes in a former cycle components factory at Hozier Street, in Bridgeton, and Norman Fulton with T Blackwood Murray completed the first production Albion chassis by June. Like Johnston, with whom they had worked at different times, these prudent engineers made as much as possible in their own workshop.

Govan took a more up-to-date point of view; his early cars were voiturettes and not dogcarts, which were already out of date: they were soon available in different powers of engine, they were light in weight and quite manageable. His rivals, Albion and Arrol-Johnston, were still stuck with their dogcart, but Albion had already taken a strong hint from the local motoring press and was going ahead with a new type of engine and chassis. Arrol-Johnston, their engine apart, were wedded to end-of-century automobile engineering and it was 1905 before they moved into the 20th century.

Within a couple of years Govan was able to offer a range of models wider than anyone else's in Scotland. He was able to up-date his chassis. He was able to rationalise the engines, importing most of them from France for a long time. He was even able to fit his own design of gearbox - though

Belhaven lorry c1910, built in Wishaw by Robert Morton & Sons

that had many critics! No one else could match him on his home ground for sheer variety. This was to lead to eventual difficulties in marketing, however.

George Johnston was the first known Scottish importer of a car, bringing it in on 18th October 1895. Almost two months later T R B Elliot of Kelso, a local landowner, imported a Panhard phaeton.

A 3½hp Stirling-Panhard of 1899

Elliot had about twenty cars in all and continued to enjoy motoring as an amateur, protected to a considerable extent by his position in society. Elsewhere in Scotland these was quite a lot of professional interest but most of it came to nothing in the end. Only Johnston, helped for a time by his cousin, Norman Fulton, and then by T Blackwood Murray, made significant progress. Johnston and Blackwood Murray had worked on an electric alternative to the petrol car, as much of the latter's earlier training had been of an electrical kind so that he was well qualified to help. But they abandoned the idea well before concentration of their efforts on production of a petrol car began around 1898.

Generally speaking, electricity was preferred to the internal combustion engine during most of this period. However, during 1896 and 1897 there were two exceptions. Almost at the end of 1896 *The Scottish Cyclist* published two reports on a Dundee venture that quickly came to nothing. It began with a display of one or two parts of the vehicle in a showroom window; the vehicle itself went on public display in the city centre.

Arrol-Johnston three-cylinder model at one time in the famous Sword collection (George Oliver archive, Museum of Transport)

> *It was driven by an oil engine, it was to be capable of up to 16 mph and to be capable of carrying from 5 to 6 tons.*

> *The Patentees, Messrs Ross and Alexander, claimed that it would be the first motor-car, every part of which had been made in this country.*

The car was a large one, in form resembling a lorry, the motive power derived from petroleum, and the wheels constructed on the cycle principle, rubber tyred.

Madelvic electric brougham, produced by William Peck at Granton, near Edinburgh

> *Named the Dei-Donum the car attracted the greatest curiosity when it appeared in the central part of the city. Its progress however, was inglorious and revealed all sorts of defects and objections. A total lack of smoothness in its motion was evident, while there was both noise and smell in abundance. Latterly, after a procession at a funeral pace, with spasmodic stoppages, the motor-car eventually sat down and all efforts to restart it proved unavailing.*

Horses towed it away. At the beginning of 1897, again according to *The Scottish Cyclist*

> *A Dunfermline-built motor-car is presently on view at the premises of Messrs Michael Tod & Son, Devon Engine Works, Dunfermline. Both motor and car have been built at these works, the furnishings being supplied by a local coachbuilder. It is a three-wheeler; two driving and a steering wheel in front. It is seated for four persons and weighs about 10 cwt .....the fuel used is petroleum and it is*

Alley and MacLellan Sentinel wagon of 1912, built in Glasgow

expected to travel on a good road at up to 22 mph. The patent is held by a Glasgow gentleman and the builder. The firm have half a dozen of the same to go on with immediately.

This last was quite untrue.

In December of the previous year - 1896 - the McDonald brothers, of Strathtay, had turned out a quadricycle, worked by their primary battery. Its 30in wheels were fitted with 2in Scottish pneumatic tyres and driven by a $^3/_4$hp motor, geared with a worm wheel on the centre of the rear shaft, with a 30 to 1 ratio. The twenty cells of the battery were carried, fifteen under the seat, on either side of the motor, and five in a covered case in front of the seat. Each cell weighed 8 lb and the entire engine weighed $3^1/_2$ cwt. It needed only salt and water for re-charging and $12^1/_2$ mph was possible - perhaps even more on a good, level road. Further tests were reported in 1897 but after that nothing more was heard of the McDonalds or their storage battery.

On 27th March 1897, Messrs Morton & Co, of Wishaw, applied for a warrant to erect buildings to be used for a motor-car and cycle works. A week or two later Mr Bremner, of the company, informed *The Scottish Cyclist* that Morton had built its first motor-car and that it had undertaken very satisfactory trials. The car had been sent north, to Strathspey. It was seated for two persons and was fitted with one of the British Motor Syndicate's electric motors.

In February 1897, the Neale electric car was announced. It was constructed of varnished wood, by John Drew & Co, of Belford Road, Edinburgh, and had four wheels.

> *It was very like a chapel cart, it weighed 7 cwt and was claimed to be the lightest motor-car in the world. There were no chains, the 1 hp motor working direct by means of a cog wheel on a ratchet wheel. There were only two levers, one for steering and the other for controlling the brake and switch. The car presented a particularly neat appearance and was totally unlike the typical motor-car, being indeed just like a horse-drawn vehicle minus the shafts. It was fitted with electrical apparatus by Mr G V Middleton, London and Edinburgh.*

Dalhousie two-seater, manufactured by the Anderston-Grice Co Ltd of Carnoustie (George Oliver archive, Museum of Transport)

Stirling bus, produced at the former Madelvic Works about 1902

On 3rd March 1897

> *...two Aberdeen motor-car dealers... were willing to place two of their cars at the disposal of the Links and Cars Committee provided the Council supplied free electricity...If the experiment was successful, the coachbuilder would supply a conveyance to seat 24 in all, at a cost of 300 guineas, with a guarantee of several years.*

Nothing came of this or of other schemes for a bus service to the beach, but it was pursued for quite a time by the Links and Cars Committee. Almost certainly an interested party would have been John F Clark, one of the city's leading coachbuilders, who was experimenting with electric propulsion at that time (he had two vehicles on trial and he may have made one or two more).

In 1897 John Stirling launched his Stirling cars, advertising that he would take orders for Dogcarts, Stanhopes, Victorias, Wagonettes and Vans, with delivery from late April onwards. He had made two contracts with the Daimler Motor Co of London, on 30th December 1896, and again on 4th and 5th December 1897, and this probably took care of most of his chassis needs. Someone did report seeing almost a score of Pennington-Stirlings in the factory, early in 1899, but, because of what one knows of Pennington, this is a highly improbable tale.

The company was not formally established until 9th December 1897: John Stirling himself indicated that he was no chassis designer, and that he bought in his frames and mechanism complete, ready for the coachbuilder (in this case his family concern) to buckle on the body of one's choice. Until 1900 he did well: after that his sales dropped swiftly as Argyll production increased, and a move to Granton and an attempt to break into bus production came rather too soon.

In 1897 the 'Craigievar Express' was completed. It had taken its builder 'Postie' Lawson, the postmaster at Craigievar in Aberdeenshire, the best part of two years to build, missing the Queen's Jubilee by only a week or so. It was steam-driven, with a boiler from England, and an engine and fittings from an Aberdeen source. Its main framing, including the seats, was of local pine. Although it missed the Jubilee celebrations, it did run from time to time, largely at galas and other social occasions. Steering was its biggest problem. The inventor of this tricycle retired it in 1934 but it did run again, even if rarely. In the late 60s it was moved from Craigievar Castle, where it had been for many years in the care of Lord Sempill, to the South. There, in the hands of its new owner, Maurice Smith, latterly Editor of *The Autocar*, it was fully restored. In November 1971 it made the journey from London to Brighton. Since the mid 80s the Craigievar Express has been an important exhibit at the Grampian Transport Museum in Alford.

The formation of the Madelvic Carriage Co on 19th January 1898, was Edinburgh's first serious involvement with the motor industry. William Peck, the city's one and only astronomer, had what seemed to him a capital idea. He planned to replace the fore-carriage of any four-wheel horse-drawn vehicle with a pair of wheels that took their power from an electric motor coupled to storage batteries in the main vehicle. There were two snags, however. In the first instance there was already some doubt about its long-term future so far as the horse-drawn vehicle was concerned and in the second the storage battery, as it was known in the 90s, was generally unreliable. Although Peck managed to obtain a contract from the Postmaster General in Edinburgh in May 1899 to carry mail between the General Post Office and Leith, its success was not long-lasting.

Peck's company had a capital of £25,000. He spent £35,000 on a custom-built factory complete with test track, and by summer 1899 was

Belhaven charabanc

attempting to raise another £25,000. No one would subscribe any more and by December the concern was in liquidation. It was the first failure: it was not to be the last.

Elsewhere in Scotland there was activity: in Aberdeen the Harper car was in production, spasmodically, from the late 90s until 1905 or thereabouts. In Stirling John Simpson had been experimenting with steam since 1897 and seemed by 1900 to have resolved most, if not all, of his problems. The Simpson steam-car had four cylinders, with one speed for the two-seater and two on the larger machine. The smaller weighed about 12 cwt. Few sales were made.

It is a remarkable fact that more was not done to exploit steam as a motive source. James Watt from Greenock positively discouraged his assistant, James Murdoch, from developing a road-going steam vehicle, wanting nothing of it. At different times during the 19th century Scottish inventors interested themselves in steam-driven carriages, buses and traction engines, the most successful of the last being the Thomson. This was made in some numbers and was in service well into the 20th century.

In and around Glasgow there was already enormous knowledge of practical applications of steam for marine engines and for most other purposes and it must not be forgotten that one of the great centres for steam locomotive building was Springburn, in Glasgow. Only in goods transport was the use of steam really successful; the Stewart-Thornycroft lasted from 1902 to 1916 and the Sentinel in Scotland from 1902 to 1915; Morton turned out the occasional Belhaven lorry or bus well into the new century and Halley began with steam, switching to petrol, however, before long.

In 1900 John Tavendale of Laurencekirk acquired a 3 hp water-cooled engine in kit form and built it into a finished unit. This he coupled to a chassis but it was not a success, the engine lacking sufficient power to drive a four-seater and the extreme vibration of engine and gearbox making them unreliable. He tried again, this time with a 6 hp Accles-Turrell motor, to which some improvements had been made, and there was a notable improvement in performance. But the St Laurence was not a commercial success.

In 1900 also, the Cassel and the Kingsburgh were introduced: I know very little about either of them except that the Cassel came from Glasgow and was available in different powers, and the Kingsburgh was built in very small numbers in the Granton works that had been sold to its makers in 1900 after the liquidation of the Madelvic Carriage Co.

On the second last day of 1899 a firm was founded in Glasgow whose name was to spread world-wide within only a few years.

Albion Motors' South Street premises under construction

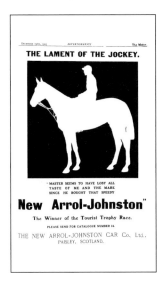

*Advertisement for Arrol-
Johnston (The Motor)*

*Chassis detail of Arrol-
Johnston 24hp of 1924
(photograph The Motor)*

As a private firm, the Albion Motor Car Company was established by
T Blackwood Murray and Norman Fulton, who, at different times during
the second half of the 90s, had worked with George Johnston. Fulton left
to widen his knowledge and experience of automobile engineering in
North America; Blackwood Murray, however, held on to his position as
works manager until 1899 when the most tactful time was chosen for his
resignation and for the setting-up of the partnership with Fulton - a move
long planned by the pair and by Murray's father.

At the same time as he was completing plans for the production of the
first Arrol-Johnston cars, Blackwood Murray was well advanced with
design work on the first Albion, this being carried out in transatlantic
letters between himself and Fulton. The latter and Murray's father were
kept fully informed about the problems of working with Johnston, who
could be very difficult to get along with as they already knew. There were
one or two false alarms before the news was finally broken to Johnston
that his dogcarts were to have rivals. In the event he raised no objections
and even offered to help if he could. Fulton returned from America, a
modest workshop was rented from the Clan Line at Finnieston Street,
Glasgow, a small staff was assembled and spent the first six months of
1900 putting together the first production Albion.

It had a somewhat scrappy look to begin with because it was fitted with
narrow section pneumatic tyres but these were soon replaced by solids
and the production dogcarts, from 1900 onwards, were greatly improved

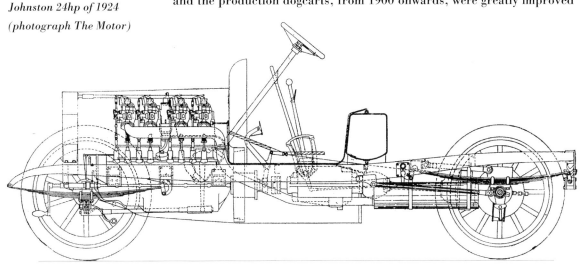

*Chassis of the new Arrol-Johnston 24h.p. four-cylinder vertical engine, transverse rear springs, 14 gallon petrol tank under
front seats, etc., etc.*

in appearance as a result. Indeed many of the early production Albions had a slightly sporting look. They would have responded very well to the sort of superfine finish featured on all the Arrol-Johnston dogcarts that I have ever seen. The latter had more of the horseless-carriage in their appearance overall.

Even with its clothes on it is obvious that the Albion is robust. In essence the frame members of the Albion closely resemble those of an iron bedstead, but they are somewhat heavier and somewhat stronger too, as may be seen from the chassis of the first Albion which survives in Glasgow's Museum of Transport. Yet there is no great excess of weight; the axles are of modest dimensions and the tiller steering is of simple construction; a radius-rod on either side at the rear locates the rear axle, which is driven by a single chain and springing is by four full-elliptic

Above

Early Albion 8hp 10cwt commercial vehicle

Right

Albion official photograph of a bus delivered to an Egyptian school about 1924

Above
*Albion lorry which spent all
its working life in the Orkney
Islands, photographed in
Museum of Transport,
Kelvin Hall, 1988*

Right
*An early view of the Albion
works at South Street,
Scotstoun*

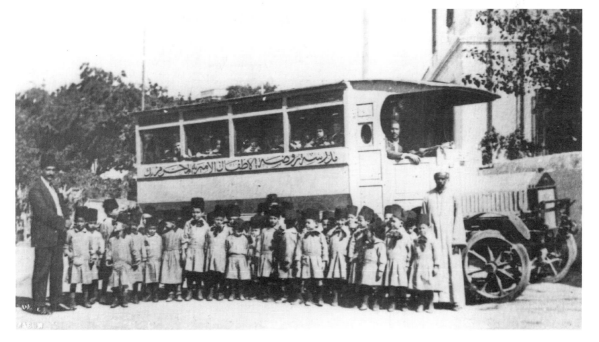

Above: *Scene at Finnieston Street works of the Albion Company about 1900*
Left: *Typical Albion lorry of the late 1920s restored and photographed at a rally at Glamis Castle (George Oliver archive, Museum of Transport)*

springs. In all these respects the Albion and the Arrol-Johnston closely match one another; as one might expect in the circumstances since as works manager of the Mo-Car Syndicate Blackwood Murray had been intimately involved with the latter.

Where the cars differed greatly was in the design of their engines. Five men built the first chassis; two years later forty-three men were responsible for making thirty-three 8hp chassis and two 10hp chassis and T Blackwood Murray and Norman Fulton, were joined on the Board by J F Henderson. The Albion Motor Car Co was turned into a limited company in 1902, had increased its capital from the modest £1,550 with which it began, its output, its markets worldwide and its reputation. As a company it was run on text-book lines, basically conservative but most active and effective on the sales side. The mechanical simplicity and reliability of its cars, lorries and buses were a strong sales factor, of course.

The rightness of its design was confirmed by a leap in output to twenty-one in 1901 and growing demand led to the building of a sizeable factory at Scotstoun in 1903, with later extensions. In 1914, with production concentrated on goods and bus chassis, output was 591 vehicles. By then Albion was selling strongly worldwide.

Almost 6,000 32hp lorries were supplied to the War Office during the First World War and after it survivors were bought back, properly reconditioned, then sold. This wise policy (followed also by Leyland) was typical of the company's responsible attitude. In design a deliberately conservative line was taken; reliability and longevity, along with high standards of care and repair, mainly through the depot system, had priority at all times.

Between the Wars bus sales grew substantially, especially to Scottish operators, and the design of a wide range of commercials kept pace with changes in users' needs and in legislation.

Albion at war, World War 1 scenes

Group including Albion, Arrol-Johnston and Argyll at the Museum of Transport, Albert Drive, Glasgow

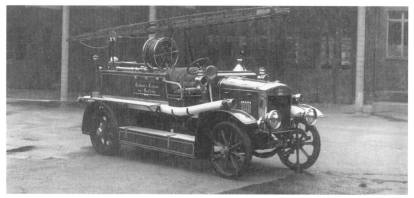

Albion-Merryweather fire engine, type D chassis

1935 Albion at work

The Albion outlived all its Scottish contemporaries, staying independent until 1952, when it was taken over by British Leyland. With consistently wise management and products of sustained quality it did not suffer the financial ups and downs of some rivals and after 1919 continued to prosper. It was the only consistently successful builder of motor vehicles in Scotland. The Albion set a standard of commonsense in the design of its products, of excellence in their construction and of exemplary management which, if followed by its few competitors, might have kept them in business too...

The new Underwood works in Paisley c1908 of the new Arrol-Johnston Car Co Ltd

To summarise: in the last two years of last century, Scotland had the makings of a motor industry. Only Albion, however, survived the two World Wars: all the others, including British Leyland and Rootes, which were brought in by the government after the Second World War, and a few very small companies, went into liquidation sooner or later.

Chapter Two

Manufacturing in Scotland Develops and Declines *1900 - 1918*

Between 1889 and 1900 George Johnston was putting the finishing touches to the Arrol-Johnston dogcart and had found somewhere to make it. He began production in a small factory that had previously belonged to the father of Peter Burt, whose name will recur in connection with the Argyll single-sleeve valve engine at a later point in this narrative. It was at Camlachie, in the East End of Glasgow, but only a few cars were made there before catastrophe struck. Early in 1901 a fire consumed the works, the cars under construction at the time and all the records and drawings - which is one reason why it is almost impossible to learn anything about the early years of this company.

It was 1902 before manufacture began again, at Underwood, in Paisley, where accommodation had been found in a disused thread mill belonging to the Coats concern. Members of the family, it will be remembered, had considerable holdings in the Mo-Car Syndicate, the company that made the Arrol-Johnston. As early as 1904 John S Napier was listed as general manager and secretary and one wonders when it was that George Johnston left the scene. Until then the archaic look of the Arrol-Johnston had prevailed; it was of the 19th and not the 20th century in its appearance and only its engine showed any signs of progressive thinking. The latter was good enough to last until 1905 at least, and was fitted to vans until well after that. It was of the four piston, horizontally-opposed type, located at the rear of the chassis and of a singularly neat appearance. Each of the two cylinders actually contained two pistons that were connected by a short rod to a rocking lever working on a bearing. This lever, at its lowest end, drove the crankshaft by means of a connecting rod. Although the engine had only two cylinders, the four pistons and their connections meant that because each explosion was of

Left

Advertisement for Arrol-Johnston

the double-acting kind the crank was pushed in two places and not in one. The result, when it was properly tuned, was smooth running, a fact I was able to confirm during a run in a 1902 dogcart in the late 1960s. It made a fair commotion when starting but once it was warm the action of its mechanism passed almost unnoticed.

As I said at the time in a motoring journal

> *Certainly a dominating impression is one of smooth and easy movement, as if one's mount were borne on liquids and not on land. Once under way the impression is still overwhelmingly nautical; apart from its easy motion this car moves forward with such relative quietness and lack of effort that one refers again to sea-going experience for comparative purposes. One is aware of mechanism at work - somewhere; just where is difficult to determine with any accuracy, however, because of the general smoothness and lack of any obvious point-source of sound. Under acceleration there is a remote flurry of muffled mechanical commotion, just as in an old-time motor-launch; but once top gear and a steady speed have been reached all is calm and peaceful once more. The contrast between his lack of fuss and the relative clatter of slowly moving parts on starting is remarkable. With experience one discovers that it is characteristic, the engine and adjacent parts quietening down as they warm to their work.*

Incidentally, the other lasting impression was of the comfort of the car, in spite of its solid tyres and its quite short full-elliptic springs. Perhaps Johnston was right when he claimed that the tyres he used were of a superior kind.

In his use of a force-feed lubrication system he was much ahead of his time. The oil pump was situated low down in the sump and the gear driven from the half shaft. Apart from the oil fed by the pressure to the crank-shaft bearings and the little-ends, for example, there was an oil-splash tray fitted below the crankshaft for spray lubrication of other parts.

The inlet valves were of the automatic kind. An Arrol-Johnston low-tension magneto was fitted. The gearbox had four forward speeds and reverse and was highly praised at the time. Final drive was by a single chain. In the original dogcarts the brakes were of the spoon type and of

22

1922 Arrol-Johnston 15.9 hp all-weather tourer outside entrance to the former Heathhall factory. The car has a body constructed by Penman of Dumfries (photograph George Oliver archive, Museum of Transport).

limited value in wet weather. At the speeds at which these cars would be largely driven this was probably of little consequence. Nevertheless, I once paced the Lithgow car at almost 40mph, a speed it maintained with ease.

To begin with there were two versions of the dogcart - a 10 hp, four-seater and a 12hp, six-seater - for which much of the bodywork was made by Wylie & Lochhead, a well-known firm of cabinetmakers in Glasgow. The finish of all the dogcarts that I have ever seen has been of the highest quality - varnished mahogany woodwork, with leather seats of a contrasting colour and a discreet use of polished brass. In four or five years of production they changed little; mostly they were open, although I did once photograph a 12hp with a canopy, on a London-Brighton run. In May 1903, incidentally, *The Motor Car World*, in a description of the Underwood factory, stated that output was then at least four cars per week with ten possible.

In 1904 (perhaps even earlier) George Johnston stole a march on Alex Issigonis by building a three-cylinder Arrol-Johnston with its engine mounted transversely across the front of the frame and set to slope backwards slightly. It was of conventional design, the outer cylinders being of $4^{1}/_{4}$in bore and the centre one of $4^{3}/_{4}$in for best balance. The crankshaft transferred power to the gearbox via a silent chain and in the gearbox was also mounted the coil clutch, running in oil. The final drive was by Renold's silent chain. The engine gave 20bhp at 80rpm. As *The Engineer* said, at the end of its description of the car

> *The workmanship and material used in the production of the Arrol-Johnston carriage give the impression of sound engineering knowledge.*

Fine finish and general neatness were notable features.

In 1903 Arrol-Johnston had entered several of their cars for Reliability Trials at Crystal Palace, London. Because of misdirection, however, they arrived too late and were refused admission. Miss Murison, an Irish girl who knew George Johnston and who happened to be there, offered to drive one of the cars part of the way back to London. The persons from Paisley accepted her offer with qualifications, and she found herself committed to drive the car from Land's End to John O'Groats instead! For someone who had not previously driven the car there was time only for an hour or two of instruction before she set out for the 900-mile run. The distance was covered in five days, the longest daily run being 213 miles. Photographs taken at John O'Groats show three cars in the team, all, it would seem, in excellent condition at the end of their extended run. One assumes that this was the number taking part. According to the *John O'Groats Journal* Miss Murison accomplished the journey without the slightest hitch; a considerable feat, if so, for any of the team, whatever the sex.

On 21st September 1905, William Beardmore of Parkhead Forge, Glasgow, took over the Mo-Car Syndicate, with a capital - on paper at least - of £100,000. The original directors were William Beardmore, John Hunter and John S Napier, each of whom had a £500 holding in the new company. The Mo-Car Syndicate had lost money (how much will never be known) and the new did too; in 1906 £22,269 7s 11d and in 1907 £40,170 7s 9d. These were relatively large sums of money, even by much later standards.

From: The John O'Groats Journal, 9th October 1903

A MOTORING FEAT

Miss Murison, a young Irish lady, has succeeded in driving a party of ladies and gentlemen, with their luggage, from Land's End to John O'Groats. the tour was commenced at 4pm on 22nd September, and John O'Groats was reached on Monday afternoon. The nett running time was 57$\frac{1}{2}$ hours for over 900 miles, being an average speed of 15$\frac{1}{2}$ miles per hour. Miss Murison drove the whole distance unaided. The feat is the more remarkable considering that she first stepped on a motor-car only a few weeks ago, and since then, she has had less than a dozen lessons in driving. The Arrol-Johnston car which she had is simple in its working, and easily handled. Miss Murison, who returned to Inverness on Tuesday following, completed the drive of a thousand miles within the week.

As a matter of interest Sir William Arrol received £18,000 as his share of the purchase price, with much smaller shares going to other directors. By 30th April 1912 it would appear that 3,419 shares had been taken up, representing £34,190. This was far short of the declared capital of £100,000.

The new Arrol-Johnston Company Ltd seemed to care as little about making money as its predecessor. It made no attempt to modernise the appearance of its passenger cars until 1905 and even after victory in the Tourist Trophy race in the Isle of Man of that year, no serious attempt was made to market TT replicas. There is, in the Museum of Transport in Glasgow, a splendid example that would surely have sold well had it been available in any quantity. It almost seemed as if Beardmore wanted his cars to lose money, and it was not until 1909, when T C W Pullinger came up from Humber, that there seemed to be a change of mind on profit-making. In a very short space of time, indeed, red figures were turned to black.

In 1905, the year of the takeover, Arrol-Johnston appeared to be in good heart. Under John Napier's direction the 12hp chassis had been completely redesigned and now looked like most other cars: it had a radiator at the front, a low bonnet, a steering column, seats and it ran on pneumatic tyres fitted to wire wheels. The engine, up-rated to 18hp but still of Johnston's late 90s design - was now housed at the front of the frame, set well back. Final drive was by four-speed gearbox and a short propeller-shaft, and there were radius rods to locate the rear axle. Two cars were entered for the Tourist Trophy race, differing only in colour.

Four complete circuits of the course had to be completed at an average fuel consumption of 22.5 mpg and there was a weight limit of 2,550 lb. Napier led for most of the way in a race that eliminated twenty-three of the fifty-four cars taking part, and won at an average speed of 33.9mph. Northey, who was driving a 20hp Rolls-Royce, was second, at 33.6mph and the other Arrol-Johnston, driven by E J Roberts, was fourth.

In 1906 Napier again entered two cars, one in the Light Touring Car race, the other in the Heavy Touring Car race. This time he was quite out of luck, neither car finishing. The weather was appalling and it is a wonder that as many as two cars completed the race. The winning car was a Rover and its makers were quick to exploit its success, putting a TT replica on the market within a month of their victory. It differed little from the winning car - artillery wheels instead of wire, a longer wheel-base and a choice of three or four speeds.

There had been resistance to the idea of the dogcart throughout its production life, regardless of the reliability of its engine. In 1904, at the time of the Edinburgh Motor Show, *The Motor Car World* had this to say

> *The Mo-Car Syndicate have the means, the technical and mechanical knowledge, and the equipment to be running the Wolseley Company close for output of cars in the United Kingdom, if they build according to accepted ideas, which, after all, is only the survival of the fittest, but they will never attain to that position while they continue to manufacture the present type of car.*

By 1905, as we know, the dogcart's day was done but the engine was to be used for another two years at least, in commercial chassis (perhaps the three-cylinder as well). During 1907 the company was building boats and it may well be that the twin-cylinder, four piston, was used to power those.

Two cars were entered once more in the 1907 TT race - a 25hp in the Light Touring Car event and a 38-45hp - a new model - in the race for Heavy Touring Cars. Neither completed the course: Napier, driving the 25hp car, broke his front axle and a wheel, and Roberts, in the 38-45hp, broke a universal joint. A year later three Arrol-Johnstons were entered for the Fourth Race in the Isle of Man and, yet again, they were out of luck. On looks alone they deserved to win but they had been prepared too quickly: in a letter to *The Motor Car World* in November 1908 Ernest A Rosenheim (who was by then general manager of Arrol-Johnston) said that there had been insufficient time to incorporate improvements 'learned from participation in the Fourth race.' This, presumably, explained his company's absence from the Olympia show that year. I am inclined to believe that their fortunes were low - really low - by then and that Beardmore was being pressed hard to find someone who could turn loss into profit.

Arrol-Johnston had always had a nose for the unconventional. In 1905 they made a dogcart for desert use, with special disc wheels, a canopy to protect its occupants and a Mavor & Coulson searchlight on a trailer, powered almost certainly by a take-off from the car engine. If I am not mistaken it was built to the order of Sir Francis Wingate, father of Orde Wingate of Second World War fame, for service in the Sudan.

In 1907 he ordered a second car for long-distance patrols in the deserts of Egypt (he was now the Sirdar), choosing a car of much more conventional appearance, with a 45hp engine that could develop as much as 75bhp on demand. Because it was enclosed in metal sheets it was absolutely sand-proof. The road wheels, which were shod with solid tyres, carried discs of steel bolted on each side and paddle blades were fixed to the driving wheels to aid traction over exceptionally soft sand. Seven people could be accommodated in the body which was made of metal sheets supported on a steel frame. Ample supplies of water and provisions were carried.

In the same year a car was built for Lieutenant Shackleton RN, who was leading a party to the South Pole. He was a friend of Beardmore, who arranged for a sinecure to be paid to him beforehand (£20 a month, I believe) and made him a present of the car once it was finished. It had a Simms four-cylinder air-cooled engine and the exhaust pipe from one of the cylinders went straight into the carburettor mixing-chamber jacket before entering the silencer. It then fed into a foot-warmer on the toe-board and finally passed through a melting tank that converted snow into drinking water. Although it was said that Arrol-Johnston's drawing-office staff knew little about polar exploration and Shackleton little about the motor-car it was a success. Bernard Day did the driving.

Arrol-Johnston sledge built for Shackleton's 1905 expedition

The Motor Car World put it rather neatly in 1910

> *Without doubt Johnston, who, together with Sir William Arrol, gave the Arrol-Johnston its name, was a mechanical genius, but, unfortunately, he was too much of a visionary to make commercial success of his undertaking. With the advent of Mr John S Napier, and his victory in the first TT race, the name of Arrol-Johnston once more loomed large, and an excellent series of models was produced, but even yet an untoward fate seemed to hang over the old thread mills in the Underwood Road, Paisley. When Mr Napier left for Coventry the Arrol-Johnston Car Company was doing but little more than living on its reputation. The announcement that Mr T C Pullinger, of Beeston fame, was to take full command at Paisley once more raised the hopes of all that the Paisley firm would again take its place in Scottish industry to which its long and honourable career entitles it. And we have not been disappointed.*

Perhaps not more than half a dozen men connected with the Scottish motor industry at that time were professionals in every sense of the word and Pullinger was most certainly one of them. After early work experience at Chelsea Arsenal he had gone to Paris where he learned all about self-propulsion on two wheels and four, and in the early 1900s he returned to this country to salvage the Sunbeam car first of all, then to establish the Humber Company on a secure footing.

Pullinger arrived in April 1909; by June it was known that he had an entirely new car on the stocks, and by October it was launched. It closely resembled the contemporary Renault, with its coal-scuttle bonnet placed in front of the radiator. Without doubt the resemblance was deliberate, though it must be said that Arrol-Johnston had used a similar type of bonnet on the Shackleton car of 1907. The engine and gearbox shared a common aluminium bedplate which made for great rigidity, especially at the front end of the frame, where extra strength must have been appreciated as long as four-wheel brakes were fitted. These, incidentally, were of the Allen-Liversidge pattern; with proper care they worked well enough but, as George Cutbush once said: 'I...remember that they provided some fine front wheel skids if carelessly used.' By 1912 they had been dropped. Argyll persevered with their four-wheel braking until 1914, and would have brought it back after the war had they been able to afford to do so.

The new 15.9, as it was known, followed conventional practice. Its four-cylinder engine was highly accessible and of neat appearance: it was also powerful enough to take the quite large car up to 40mph or so. It was popular from the start and soon Underwood (which had been quite badly damaged in a fire in September 1909) began to feel the strain. In addition to the new car there were two commercial chassis in production and in 1911 a six cylinder 23.9 chassis was introduced. Moreover a smaller 11.9 had been announced by the Olympia Show. This had been designed, like the 15.9, by the chief draughtsman Biggs, and was introduced to Scottish motorists early in 1912. Before Olympia an 11.9 averaged 50.52 mph for

*Glasgow-built Argyll 1904
with chauffeur (photograph
Robert Grieves)*

6 hours at Brooklands and made a best lap of 56 mph, high speeds for such a small car at that time. The 23.9, which could carry large and luxurious bodywork because of its power and size, was discontinued towards the end of 1913 and replaced by a 20.9, four cylinder chassis. For 1915 a new 17.9 was announced and the 11.9 was dropped.

Before that time there had been one last attempt to succeed in the French light car race at Boulogne, with three 15.9 cars suitably modified. There was no victory but Reid was seventh, Dario Resta eighth and Hodge eleventh, and in 1912 three more modified 15.9s were entered for the French Grand Prix. Although there had been some experiments with an overhead-camshaft engine it was decided in the end to continue with the standard side-valve 80x150 unit. Two of these engines were fitted to short wheelbase (8ft 6in) chassis and the third to an even shorter one - 8 ft in fact. Two of the cars had live axles while the third was chain-driven. Five-speed gearboxes were fitted, fifth gear being an indirect. The race was over in two days (which may have given the French spectators time to get used to the Gordon tartan finish of the cars...) and only Wyse finished - ninth overall and fifth in the 3-litre class.

Later in the year another team of Arrol-Johnstons was entered for the French Grand Prix but in the event they failed to start. Pullinger's primary concern was with touring cars but he had been involved in competitive motoring at an earlier stage in his career, having been in charge of the assembly of the Weir-Darracq racing cars in Glasgow, in 1904, and having been responsible for the Beeston-Humbers that took part in the 1905 Isle of Man Touring Trophy.

By 1910 the new Arrol-Johnston Company was in a much more secure financial state that it had probably ever been before. Its profit for the year was £5,957; it claimed that it was producing upwards of 18 cars every week at Underwood and that orders for 1911 and 1912 were more than double previous figures. I do not dispute the profit: I do dispute output, however, this being the figure most often exaggerated, and I would put the real number at around 450. Whatever it was it caused production problems at Paisley. No one was very surprised when Arrol-Johnston announced that they were going to move to Heathhall, a couple of miles from Dumfries, as soon as a thoroughly up-to-date factory had been built there. At Underwood, meanwhile, it was claimed that over 600 cars per annum were being produced by 1912-13.

A new company was registered on 1st May 1912, with a capital of £100,000 in £1 shares, and two directors only - William Beardmore, who had £21,000 invested, and T C W Pullinger, who had £7,000. The old company had done well in 1910 and 1911 and by the end of 1914 the new one was doing even better, showing a profit of £21,128 18s 5d. According to one set of figures that I have, profit-making continued until 1924, when it was £9,546 12s 1d; in 1925 it had turned into a heavy loss, with £37,749 4s 7d on the debit side.

But before the war all was well; the range was a good one and output was increasing, an electrically-driven car was being made at Underwood in 1913 and there was still a limited production of commercial and bus chassis: meanwhile the fine new factory was going up expeditiously at Dumfries. That was extremely good value at £85,000, including land, plant, etc, built as it was on the Khan system, largely of ferro-concrete and glass, with ample room for extensions should they be needed, upwards of 80 acres being available.

Heathhall was opened at the end of July 1912, by the Marquis of Graham, with Beardmore, Pullinger and three hundred specially invited guests in attendance. Pullinger explained some of the reasons for settling in Dumfries - healthy working conditions, availability of labour, access to raw materials from the south as well as from Scottish sources, ease of transport by road and rail. He forecast that by 1914 the factory would be fully productive. What he could not foresee was that it would still be in existence in the 1990s - in good-as-new condition - and still in production, but with Wellington boots as a prime product.

Between 1910 and 1914 Arrol Johnston Limited was at its peak. It was making worthy cars and also making money: from all accounts Pullinger was a popular managing director and exceptionally friendly relations were maintained with dealers and customers. By December 1915, according to *The Motor World*, 600 men were employed, earning £1,000 per week and making four cars in that time. The firm had orders in hand for approximately one thousand cars. As production increased at Dumfries the Paisley works would be devoted to the construction of electric cars, both pleasure and commercial. By 1914, on the other hand, Argyll was finished, its former dominant position in the pleasure car business no longer tenable; no longer able to pay its way and, by June 1914, more than £70,000 in debt. This time there were no rescuers, no

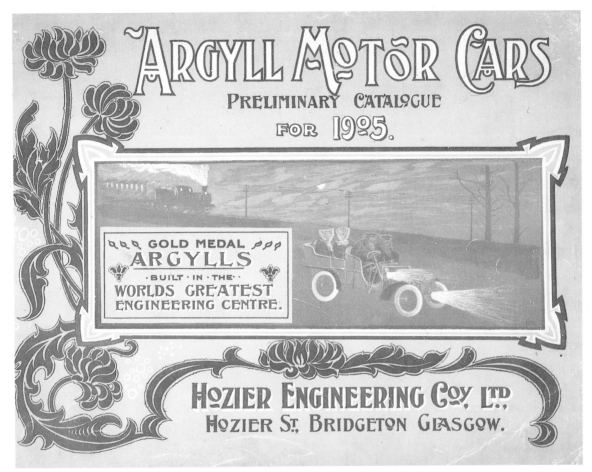

GOLD MEDAL
ARGYLLS
·BUILT·IN·THE·
WORLDS GREATEST
ENGINEERING CENTRE.

ARGYLL MOTOR CARS
PRELIMINARY CATALOGUE
FOR 1905.

HOZIER ENGINEERING COY LTD.,
HOZIER ST. BRIDGETON GLASGOW.

Argyll Motor Cars preliminary catalogue 1905, front cover

one to cast financial life-belts: but in 1917, on 14th March, a third company, the Argyll Motor Co Ltd, was registered, with J D Brimlow as managing director. It was to be given about 11 more years of active life.

Its beginnings in 1899 had been fraught enough. W A Smith, a Glasgow entrepreneur, found himself saddled with a well-equipped but bankrupt cycle components factory, the management of which had been inept, and this fact, plus a recession in the cycle trade, had caused its failure. There were rumours at the time of financial mismanagement on the part of some of those involved, which would appear to have been well founded. At any rate Smith, who knew Alex Govan in person and by local repute, consulted him about a possible use for the factory: several were suggested and by 16th October 1899, the Hozier Engineering Company was in business, in Hozier Street, Bridgeton, with Govan in charge. The

16-20 Ḧ.P. Argyll Car.

(4 CYLINDER.)

TONNEAU.

Price, = = **£550**

Price (Fitted with 3 Cylinder 12-14 H.P. Argyll Engine), **£425**

Built with extended Wheel Base and Side Doors to the Tonneau, £50 extra.

company was prepared to tackle general engineering and car repairing (not that there was likely to be much in that line for quite a while yet) and Govan made it very clear that as soon as he could he would begin to manufacture cars of his own design.

This promise was carried out with speed and by the summer of 1900 a new Argyll voiturette was described in *The Autocar* - the first of innumerable reports on the make that were to appear in this and other periodicals until 1914. Govan had a highly developed sense of publicity that was passed on after his death; Argyll's Press Office was one of the most efficient in the industry.

A story that I cannot confirm - but which sounds highly probable - appeared in an advertisement supplement to *The Autocar* of 18th

Illustration from the 1904 catalogue of Argyll cars and motor delivery vans, issued by Hozier Engineering Co Ltd

10-12 H.P. Argyll Car.

(2 CYLINDER.)

TONNEAU.

Price. = = £350
Built with extended Wheel Base and Side Doors to the Tonneau, £50 extra.

Illustration from the 1904 catalogue of Argyll cars and motor delivery vans, issued by Hozier Engineering Co Ltd

November 1905, written, with tongue in cheek to some extent, I trust, by The Southron. He began by explaining that while he was employed by Albert Eadie, a cycle builder of Redditch, Govan had had

...much singular, interesting and instructive experience there in connection with a Benz car, a Mors dogcart, and a Vallée car, bought by Mr Eadie for the purposes of experiment in determining the best type of car to set about making. Those early trials - for out of Mr Govan's own mouth we have it that they were trials indeed - the cacoethes automobilii, the germ motoric, were implanted in Mr Govan's system to fecundate and germinate as we see today.

Mr Govan declared for a motor output... Between August 1899 and March 1900, small cars built on Baby Renault lines were...

marketed, but the first big push-off, so far as output was concerned came from that astute, mercurial and far-seeing entrepreneur, Mr Chas Friswell.

Mr Govan was ranging London and other places in search of employment for his plant in Hozier Street and chanced to drop into Mr Friswell's motor depot... There Mr Govan's eye lighted on a Baby Renault, of which midget cars Mr Friswell was then selling quite a number - indeed so brisk was the demand that delivery was his only trouble; and when complaining of that fact, Mr Govan offered to build him some copies. The suggestion resulted in a firm order for twenty-five. The first Argyll turned out modified somewhat from the original model....

After several of the little cars had been delivered, some little trouble arose between the parties concerned; and like the sportsman he is, Mr Friswell agreed to hand over a cheque for everything outstanding if one of the cars could be successfully driven from Bridgeton to the Holborn Viaduct. Some days after he was rather more than astonished to find two much begrimed travel-stained wights in an earth-encrusted and road-stained Baby pull up... It was Govan and a true long-suffering friend from Glasgow aboard

Two Argyll advertisements

First illustrated Olympia show report 1905 (from The Motor)

Argyll catalogue 1904 front cover

that wee bit motor-car. The cheque was paid but thereafter the Hozier Engineering Co resolved to sell their own cars.

This suggests to me that reliability was the problem. And reliability was to remain a problem for some time to come. Govan had his share of trouble and, as The Southron quoted

> ...iron dug from central gloom,
>
> And heated hot with burning fears,
>
> And dipt in baths and hissing tears,
>
> And battered with the shocks of doom,
>
> To shape and use.

As Sir Henry Royce knew only too well metal was **the** enemy, and Alex Govan knew it too. In a most perceptive obituary of Govan that appeared in the *Glasgow Herald* on 28th May 1907, the writer said

The man who makes no mistakes makes nothing. Engineers had to be trained to a new and exacting form of machine construction, materials had to be found to withstand strains and stresses hitherto unheard of in this country for machinery, and through it all Mr Govan worked and schemed and struggled....for weeks on end he practically worked and ate and slept in the factory, solving one problem only to find another facing him.

Above and opposite, below
Argyll factory, Alexandria

As far as engines were concerned he bought them in until such time as he learned to build them himself, and because France seemed to be the best source he favoured French manufacturers.

At first he built small, on chassis that owed a good deal to cycle-frame manufacture, the machine tools for such work still being at Hozier Street, and he used a number of different sizes of engine, from 2 to 6 hp, and from De Dion and MMC to begin with. From 1902 he began to fit large engines: in that year he offered a choice of an 8hp De Dion or Simms, and in 1903 (by which time he had switched to pressed steel frames) he offered a 6 hp Aster, a 9hp De Dion, a 10hp two-cylinder Clement and a 16hp four-cylinder. In 1904, bowing to a passing fashion, he introduced a three-cylinder of his own manufacture.

Opposite, above
Argyll Factory, Alexandria nearing completion 1905/6.

In 1905 three models were marketed - a 10-12 hp two-cylinder Aster, a 12-14 hp three-cylinder and a 20-24 hp four-cylinder, the last fitted with engines built by Argyll. This was the pattern of production until 1906, when the main works was moved to Alexandria, about 20 miles to the north west of Glasgow.

As early as 1903 Hozier Street was finding difficulty in meeting demand and extra space had to be taken there, bodybuilding being the preserve of the new premises. Profits were going up and in 1902 a dividend of 5% was declared. In 1903 it was 10%. In 1904 it was claimed that 15 cars per week were going through the workshops (a figure that I cannot accept as correct, incidentally). The dividend then was 20% and by 1905 it had risen to 35% which I find suspicious; Hozier Engineering no longer existed, its place having been taken by a new and very ambitious company, Argyll Motors Limited, with a capital of £500,000, and the declaration of such high dividends must surely have encouraged further investment. In its last six months, indeed, Hozier paid 50%.

In 1904 Govan had visited the United States and the Continent to see how they went about things there: he returned greatly encouraged by the

steps taken to look after workers' comfort and took such action as he could in due course. I quote once again from the *Glasgow Herald* obituary.

> *Something of the sort has been done at Alexandria, and had he lived I have no doubt that Mr Govan would have succeeded in overcoming the wet-blanket reception accorded to some of his proposals by the people for whose benefit they were intended.*

It is interesting to note that while Alex Govan was preparing for one of the largest promotions in motoring history he was truly concerned about the provision of good working conditions for all his staff.

When Hozier Engineering was registered in March 1900 it had four directors - W A Smith (Chairman) Merchant; Alex W M Steven, Ironfounder; Alex Govan, Mechanical Engineer and John Worton, Clerk. The chances are that the matter of launching a much larger company was discussed between Smith, Steven and Govan in the main. Govan certainly visited American factories in 1904, some time ahead of the registration of Argyll Motors Limited, in March 1905, and it may be that Smith paid a visit also - although I can find no evidence of this. Whose decision it was to build on such a grand scale I have no idea; if I suspected anyone it would be Smith, but that is also something for which I have absolutely no evidence. It may well be that Govan was somewhat overwhelmed by what he saw in North America and returned with really big ideas that were to some extent supported by the others. But there were those who thought that the time was still too soon to make such a clean break with Bridgeton where disused cotton mills could be bought cheaply and labour was in ample supply.

The mania for magnitude took the new company to what was almost certainly the most ambitious car factory in the world at that time, occupying 11 acres at least of a very much larger site within a mile or so of Loch Lomond. If it had to be so far out of town it was well chosen: the main Alexandria-Balloch road passed outside and there were two railway lines close by. Moving cars was no problem and it seemed as if an adequate number of customers could be found to support the factory with a capacity of 2,000 cars a year. Nearly half the capital was invested in new offices, works and plant, operations beginning in March 1905 and continuing without break until the following summer. Wet weather delayed completion to some extent.

Argyll Workers, Alexandria

Argyll factory and workers c1907 (photograph Robert Grieves)

By the end of 1905 manufacturing operations were being transferred from Hozier Street to Alexandria as workshops were completed - a costly and time-consuming affair, however, as finished components had then to be ferried back to Glasgow to be incorporated in chassis under construction there. When a souvenir booklet was published in 1906 many of its illustrations were of the new workshop well filled with chassis, engines, bodywork, etc, which rather gives the lie to those motoring historians who claim that Alexandria always had more than its share of empty shops.

Empty they most certainly were not - but it has to be admitted that at no time during Argyll's occupation of the factory were they ever full - at best they never approached 50% of potential. Prospects seemed good enough in 1906 and they might well have improved had not Alex Govan died suddenly in May of the following year. At first it was thought that he had suffered a fatal attack of ptomaine poisoning following a meal at the Grosvenor Restaurant in Glasgow (his widow, indeed, sued that establishment): later, however, it was proved that a brain tumour had been the cause of death.

Argyll factory, Alexandria, gear assembling shop, c1908 (George Oliver archive, Museum of Transport)

Govan certainly had his worries. The effort of putting up the new factory had fallen largely on his shoulders, something that, in itself, would have been more than enough for most men. He was largely responsible for expanding existing markets to match the potential output of the new premises. To some extent at least he had to find a very large labour force in a district previously known mainly for dyeing and bleaching. In the *Glasgow Herald* obituary the writer referred to Govan's working and scheming and struggling.

> *... sometimes in spite of those within his gates, the workmen who should have rejoiced and assisted in the fostering of a new industry... Govan resented strongly certain efforts made in Glasgow to do the Company harm, but when the writer saw him off from the Central Station a couple of weeks ago on the journey on which he no doubt contracted his fatal illness his last words were "They may hamper us and annoy us for a time, but it is simply impossible for them to do us any real harm".*

It is impossible, of course, to know who had been spreading the rumours. Albion was too busy establishing its own business - and in any case it was not the sort of thing they would consider - and Arrol-Johnston, on all the available evidence, had more than enough problems of their own. The chances are that the trouble came from the wider business community; W A Smith was not liked by everyone and the scale of this new venture did not appeal to all. In 1906 Smith wrote to the *Glasgow Herald* to contradict rumours about Argyll that persisted at the time.

The rumoured closing of Hozier Street, once the new plant was in commission, he denied absolutely; as chairman he pointed out that a delay of three months in completing Alexandria, plus great pressure of orders, influenced the board to continue manufacture at Bridgeton longer than anticipated, thus placing an additional burden on the finances of the company... it was never contemplated that production should continue at two factories with probable production of 70-80 cars and vans per week (at the present average price per vehicle of something like a million and a quarter per annum) impossible to do so on present finances.

His answer to criticism that the company was not doing well was that the balance at 30th September was in a satisfactory state, and although there would be no benefit from the new works until May, actual sales up to the

Argyll light commercial vehicles c1908, with tenement houses of Govan Drive, Alexandria, named after Alex Govan, founder of the company

end of July would show at least a 60% increase. As for future business - up to the end of July contracts had been secured for about 264,000 of cars for the year ending on 30th September 1907.

In 1906 it was stated that the negotiations for an amalgamation of Argyll Motors (Ltd) and Scott, Stirling Co, of Twickenham, had now been concluded and that the new company was to be known as Argylls, and Stirling Commercial Motors Ltd. Twenty buses a week would be produced at the new factory. Unfortunately there was no truth in this claim and within a couple of years Scott, Stirling was in liquidation. That was the end of Stirling cars, lorries and buses, incidentally, and of John Stirling who, according to George Cutbush, eventually hit hard times.

At the time of Alex Govan's death Argyll production was much below its potential, and that, in itself, must have been causing him great worry. Almost a year from the date of his death the company went into Voluntary Liquidation, with a deficit of more than £360,000, and I find it hard to accept the statement that no one connected with the concern had any knowledge of what was happening.

By June 1908, when many - but not all - of Argyll's financial troubles were revealed, the news was of a catastrophic kind. A great deal of money had disappeared since the formation of the new company in

Albion delivery van for Thomas Lipton (photograph Robert Grieves)

March 1905 and no adequate reply was forthcoming to those who asked why. The sums of money involved were so great, in fact, that a rescue operation had to be mounted very quickly. There as a capital reduction and the assets were written down to less than half what they stood at in the books. A fresh issue of capital was authorised and the new company had something like £100,000 clear, free of old debts to set it on its way. Eventually even that was not enough.

Without any doubt Alex Govan's death was a major tragedy that affected a great many people. Probably those who felt it most were the floor staff at Alexandria, well over 1,000 of whom lost their jobs in 1908, the majority not regaining them when things began to improve. J P Christian, who had been an indentured apprentice with the Argyll Company and had served it in all the shops, wrote of the make in the *Veteran Car Club Gazette* between 1955 and 1956. One of the features of this series of articles is its author's quotation of credible output figures for many of the years reviewed. During 1909, for example, in nine months trading, the total had fallen to 240. In 1910, on the other hand, it

Above

Argyll factory, Alexandria, chromotype postcard (George Oliver archive, Museum of Transport)

Opposite

1907 Argyll 10/12 tourer

had almost doubled, to 450. In 1913 output was up again; to 622, in a good deal less than a year's trading. By then, however, the state of the company was a major topic for discussion on the Stock Exchange in Glasgow and elsewhere and its future had already been decided. There was a war in the offing and no one seemed to want to throw any more financial lifebelts to a failing car company.

In 1909, however, failure was some way off, and the new Argyll Company had more immediate matters to attend to. It had a new managing director - John Matthew - who had been put in by the Dunlop Rubber Company, as principal creditors of the former concern. When Govan died his place as managing director had been taken by A Morris Thomson who had been sharing that post with him for some time. It was felt that he lacked sufficient seniority of the task, however, and Chairman Smith also took over as managing director until Eustace Watson, then manager of the London showroom, assumed control. Matthew was appointed in January 1909. The new Chairman was Thomas Dence A Davidson ('The Bear' - so named, perhaps, because of his size) became works manager and Henri Perrot was chief designer until 1912, when Davidson resigned; thereafter he was works manager as well. W Biscombe was sales manager and John D Brimlow was Glasgow sales manager as long as Argyll had a Glasgow showroom. On the whole it was a lively team, only too keen to prove itself.

When production began at Alexandria there were four models - the 10-12 hp two-cylinder Aster, the 12-14 three-cylinder Argyll, the 16-20 hp four-cylinder Aster and the 20-24 hp four-cylinder Aster. The number of body styles was considerable. For 1906-7 a new model was introduced - a 14-16 hp with a four-cylinder T head Argyll engine (it was really an Aster built under licence) to join the 10-12, 16-20 and 26-30 hp cars and, once more, the number of different body styles was large. Too large, in fact.

For 1907-8 there were seven different chassis and no fewer than 29 types of body. The 16-20 and 26-30 hp were retained and were available in two types - in standard and de luxe form. The latter had a 'picked engine' - in practice, one that developed more than the average brake horsepower on test - a Coats's patent Argyll carburettor and a transverse rear spring. The 12-14 hp was replaced by a 12-16 hp with a monobloc Aster engine. Incidentally, although Argyll showed a strong preference for the Aster engine there was no financial tie-up between the two companies. Finally, there was another new model - a 40 hp four-cylinder chassis with dual ignition, pump lubrication of the engine, a four-speed and reverse

A preserved 10hp two-cylinder Argyll of 1910, preserved in Argyllshire

gearbox and shaft drive, available with a 9ft 9in or 10ft 6in wheelbase. It was a fast car; 60 mph was claimed in top gear. Not many were made, however.

For its re-launch Argylls Limited had three car chassis - 12-14 hp four-cylinder, a 14-16 hp four-cylinder with separate cylinders, a 35-40 hp four-cylinder cast in pairs and a 12-16 hp four-cylinder monobloc. Additionally there were several commercial and bus chassis - adaptations of existing car chassis in most cases, the lower-powered ones carrying van bodies as a rule, with little modification. Though Argyll might be said to have specialised in fire engines and marketed a 50 hp chassis, the number made was not very large. When one was handed over to the Mayoress of Keighley, in 1909, it was christened with a bottle of champagne broken over a hub, and a presentation, by John Matthew, of two silver muffineers.

Argyll fire engine outside the Alexandria factory c1908

By 1910 Argyll was already building vans and featuring them in catalogues: I have seen the 1909 catalogue which has a centre section of four pages showing commercial vehicles - lorries, vans, fire engines, a charabanc - with prices on application. John Brimlow was involved in this side of the business, certainly while it was based in Hozier Street. Argyll exported widely (if not in very great numbers) and made much of this in their publicity, giving, indeed, an impression of greater coverage than was actually the case. As we have seen, Govan set a high standard in publicity: one of his successors was William (later Sir William) Crawford who went on to found the great London advertising agency of that name. The Argyll Press Office was obviously on excellent terms with the motoring periodicals of the day, as, indeed, were its opposite numbers of Albion and Arrol-Johnston, incidentally.

For 1910 Perrot introduced a utility model that was available in three different powers - a twin-cylinder 10 hp, a four-cylinder 20 hp (in two blocks of two) and a six-cylinder 30 hp. According to Christian the 10 sold in a very small numbers, the 20 was fairly popular and the 30 was a very doubtful proposition. Another model was to become known as the Flying Fifteen. A chassis was part of the Sword Collection and is now in the Glasgow Museum of Transport's unique gathering of Scottish cars, in a handsome state of restoration. At this time a taxi-cab chassis made use of the same engine.

For 1911 the 10, Flying Fifteen, 20 and 30 hp cars were retained, with new bodies of the 'torpedo' kind. A 12 hp was introduced, with four-wheel brakes and worm final drive - the first Argyll to have these features. The brakes had been designed by J M Rubery from whom Perrot bought the design at the time of the second liquidation. I understand that the deal cost him £200, and according to Christian, sales during 1911 showed a slight increase, to 508.

In 1911 the first of the single-sleeve valve Argylls was introduced - the 25/50 - and poppet valve models included the 12 hp, its body re-styled, the Flying Fifteen, with worm-drive (except for the two-seater which had bevel-drive) and a Colonial model with special lead-coated steel panels for the body and the high ground clearance of 10in. The 20 hp was still being produced in small numbers, as was the taxi-cab chassis.

Although Argylls had been sold to New York in 1909 their operator failed before long and sales elsewhere at no time ever reached the figures

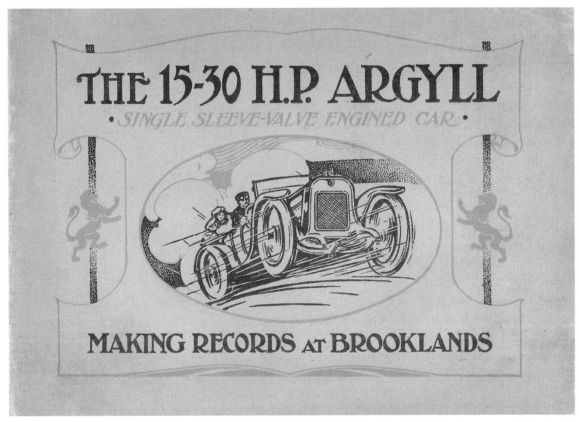

THE 15-30 H.P. ARGYLL

· SINGLE SLEEVE-VALVE ENGINED CAR ·

MAKING RECORDS AT BROOKLANDS

The front cover of a brochure produced by Argylls to mark the record breaker at Brooklands, 1913

achieved by Renault or Unic, for example. This was much less to do with the quality factor than with fashion.

In 1912 another single-sleeve was marketed - this time the 15/30, which attracted many more customers than its larger stablemate. But it was not a particularly cheap car (the Streamline Torpedo, fully equipped, cost £575) when the excellent Rover Twelve, also pretty fully equipped, cost £350. The 12 hp poppet-valve chassis and the Flying Fifteen were still in small-scale production and a 25/50 single-sleeve Colonial was specially made for Captain Kelsey who planned to drive it from the Cape to Cairo, to open up a new route. Unfortunately he was killed in a encounter with a leopard, which brought the gallant endeavour to an end.

Output for 1913 showed a slight increase, to 622, but 200 cars remained unsold and Christian did not tell us whether they were included in that figure or were over and above it. The sleeve valve chassis continued in production, scarcely changed, and there was a special Camp model, a

Colonial really, with 12in ground clearance. The taxi-cab was still listed but, again, the total made cannot have been large. Of course 1914 saw the end of Argyll, effectively speaking: by the early summer it had reached the limit of its resources and although an offer had been made by the French Darracq Company for certain of its assets, debenture holders acting through the Bank of Scotland turned that offer down. This time the deficit was in the region of £80,000 and this time there was no saviour.

Before I come to the 1914 liquidation I want to deal in some detail with the development and production of the single-sleeve valve engine. When negotiations began between John Matthew and Peter Burt, the inventor of the single-sleeve principle in this particular form, Matthew was already interested in the sleeve-valve as an alternative to the poppet. It is scarcely surprising, therefore, that agreement was reached between them; nevertheless, it was more than two years before the first production single-sleeved engine went into production. Investigations of rival, or would-be rival, systems had to be studied in detail and every possible attempt made to ensure that there was no question of infringement of patents. In the end, as we shall see, the Company was challenged on that very count.

Argyll car after the record breaking run at Brooklands (George Oliver archive, Museum of Transport)

*Peter Burt, JP, MIES
Described as the 'original
Inventor and Patentee of the
Single Sleeve Valve Engine'
as used in Argyll cars.
(Photo George Oliver
Archive, Museum of
Transport)*

Peter Burt JP had been involved with the internal combustion engine
from as far back as 1887 and his firm was well known for its stationary
oil and gas engines. In 1893 he had patented a piston-valve unit. But it
was with a model of the single-sleeve - the cylinder made of celluloid, the
sleeve of paper - that he discussed the matter with Matthew. It was
patented, provisionally, on 6th August 1909. When, however, an
application for full protection was made it was discovered that a
Canadian, J H K McCollum, had been granted British patents on 22nd
June 1909. Much further work would be required before his design could
be of any real value - but it had legally-enforceable precedence over
Burt's invention. Not without difficulty (and with some luck as well)
contact was established with McCollum in Toronto and he was invited to
meet principals of Argylls in London to resolve the problem. As it
happened he was on his way to France to discuss his patents with
Delaunay-Belville, which set another problem for Matthew to deal with
right away. But they did meet and in spite of McCollum's eccentric
behaviour during those meetings - he relied to a great extent on advice

received from his dead father and made much use of a planchette, or spirit table, to establish regular contact with the latter (a not uncommon practice, seemingly, at that time) - agreement was reached eventually, and Argylls were granted rights to the McCollum patents, the sleeve-valve engine produced thereafter being known as the Burt McCollum. There were many dealings with other inventors before Argyll felt able to go ahead. One that caused John Matthew a good deal of concern involved two individuals who had been in the company's employ (in fact one was still at work in the drawing office at Alexandria) who had patented a scheme that anticipated the company's own patent of August 1909. The whole affair sounded extremely suspicious, but it was resolved in the end.

There was yet another claimant, Edward Hoiland, of New Zealand, who was far from sight, if not from mind. During the course of discussions with American manufacturers Matthew discovered that Hoiland's representative there had been in touch with them and, as a result, they were disinclined to have anything to do with an engine so long as doubt remained about the patent rights. Then, while Matthew was in London, two items came his way, quite by coincidence. One was a copy of Hoiland's patent in *The Motor Trader*; the other was Hoiland's representative, then in London: negotiations took place and for £200 the way was cleared for Argyll to go ahead.

In the meantime work had started on the new engine. To save time, apart from anything else, an existing poppet-valve engine was used as a base, work at first being concentrated on a multi-cylinder unit. Every possible handicap seems to have been suffered at this stage yet the running of the engine really impressed those involved - even those who, like Perrot, were hostile to the idea to begin with. At first the experimental work was put in the charge of Peter Burt and his son, Thomas, and was conducted in the most thorough and painstaking manner: only minor alterations were made to the design during the production life of the engine. The Sleeve-Valve Patents Dept of Acme Wringers Ltd admitted in 1941 that, as originally designed, it was a comparatively expensive engine to make,

Left:

1913 Argyll 15/30 type G

THE SONG OF THE "ARGYLL"

O'er valley and hill like a shadow I flee,
With hardly more sound than the hum of a bee :
My wheels scarcely ever seem touching the ground,
And each little hillock I clear at a bound.
Policemen in blue at me stand aghast —
They can't see my number, I'm going so fast :
Then they look at each other and say with a smile.
"Oh, there's no need to worry, for that's an 'Argyll.'"

The children are playing all over the street,
But from me there's no danger, my steering's so neat.
My gearing's so perfect, I go as I please,
And respond to my chauffeur with consummate ease.
I can go fast or slow, or make a dead stop,
Move backwards or forwards, or spin like a top :
And for elegance, safety, and comfort and style,
There's nothing on earth to match an "Argyll".

My coat is not gaudy, but still it is chaste,
My colours are chosen with exquisite taste ;
My tyres are perfection, and when out at night,
My lamps shed around me a halo of light.
My engine's well balanced, no throbbing you feel,
And no nauscous scents on the cool breezes steal.
And if hours of pleasure away you would wile,
On a car, then be sure that you get an "Argyll".

My trials are many, but still you will see,
They nearly all end in a verdict for me ;
And the points on which jury and judge are agreed,
Are efficiency, reliability, speed.
Of medals I've plenty to wear when I choose,
Of cups, I have more than I'm able to use :
Testemonials also I've got by the mile,
All sounding the praise of the "Good old Argyll".

So if you're a millionaire loaded with wealth,
Or an adipose invalid seeking for health.
A prosperous merchant who lives out of town,
Or a shop-keeper getting your marketing down—
No matter whate're your position may be,
If you're wanting a car, have a trial of me.
And I promise that I your temper won't rile,
Or spoil the good name of the "Famous Argyll"

WM MEIKLE

Detail of sculpture above the main entrance of the Argyll works at Alexandria

requiring high standards of workmanship and special machine tools. The single-sleeve required less maintenance than a poppet-valve but it was more costly to service because of relatively poor accessibility.

The layout of the two engines (a smaller 15-30 was introduced in 1912) was the joint work of Thomas Burt and W Ferrier Brown, the latter being responsible for formulae to determine port dimensions and design with the kind of mathematical exactitude essential if satisfactory results were to be obtained. Brown was chief draughtsman at Alexandria from 1912 to 1914, and joined Daimler after the liquidation. To begin with Henri Perrot was opposed to the single-sleeve design but changed his mind once tests had proved its effectiveness and gave every possible support thereafter. He was responsible for the overall design of the 25/50, features of which, apart from its engine and worm final drive, were an efficient four-wheel braking system and much more comprehensive equipment than was usual at that time.

Almost at the beginning of production Argyll ran into trouble, however, when a writ was served on Donne and Williams who were showing, at Olympia, a Picard-Pictet fitted with a single sleeve-valve engine made under licence from Argyll. John Matthew immediately published an undertaking to indemnify all purchasers against any legal action that

might follow and asked the holders of the Knight double-sleeve patents, Messrs Knight and Kilbourne, to serve his firm with a writ also. Argylls fought the case successfully and won the appeal as well, in due course. It was alleged at the 1914 liquidation meeting that in terms of money, staff time, energy and potential sales, the actions had cost the company at least £50,000. That may very well have been the case and would account for a major part of the deficit in 1914.

In production form the engines differed little in appearance; neatness was a feature, in the Continental manner. Each block of two cylinders had its separate detachable head, secured by eight nuts, with the sparking plugs located at the centre of the combustion chambers and deep-set in the head, their pockets being sealed by vulcanite caps meant to keep out dirty water and dead insects. A Bosch magneto and a large-diameter water-pump were placed across the front of the engine, driven from the gearshaft - the latter being the equivalent of the camshaft of a poppet-valve engine. The water leads - except for those feeding directly to the cylinders - were cast integrally, which made for neatness. Lubrication was by an Albany pump of the tooth wheel type, along with splash feed to the big-ends, cylinder walls and sleeves and the gudgeon-pins.

Scottish cars in the Museum of Transport, Kelvin Hall, 1988

Left: 15.9hp Arrol Johnston 1920

Centre: 12.8hp Beardmore 1924

Right: 15/30 Argyll 1913

From the Argyll catalogue,
No 36 1914

The Argyll patent elliptical single sleeve-valve was given its vertical and partially rotatory motion by means of a sleeve-actuating disc driven by skew gears from the gearshaft that ran at half crankshaft speed and caused the sleeve to describe a complete ellipse for every turn of the engine. The connection between the actuating disc and the sleeve itself was made by a pin set eccentrically to allow it a throw of $1^{1}/_{2}$ in. In each cylinder there were three specially shaped ports for inlet and exhaust respectively, but the sleeves had five ports only, the central one in each case being of double form, to serve both inlet and exhaust.

At the top of the compression stroke, when the sleeve ports were at their highest point, they were protected by the broad lower ring carried in the cylinder head and arranged to prevent burning of the edges of the ports. During the firing stroke no edges were exposed to the incandescent gases either.

The claimed oil consumption of 1000 mpg may well have been true, and one's few memories of Argylls pre-war confirm that they were not smokers on the Daimler scale. Only one tribute to durability survives; a reader of *Motor World* who claimed that he had covered more than 40,000 miles in his 15/30 by 1914. In general the single sleeve engine improved with use, gaining in power and performance and well able to run for long periods without attention. On wonders whether it might have had a future in the taxi market had the company survived.

In May 1913, there was a public demonstration at Brooklands Race Track to prove that the 'present Argyll type of car and Argyll engine is a thoroughly sound proposition', as *The Auto* put it. Originally the idea had been to run the car for 12 hours only but it went so well that an extension of two hours was taken - and with it no fewer than 26 Class D records, from one to 14 hours, and from 50 to 1000 miles. For the duration of the run an average of 72.59 mph was maintained - a most praiseworthy performance for an engine of 2,614 cc with 2,726 lb to pull. The run was superby organised by Perrot and it was suggested by one onlooker that the Alexandria stores had been moved, temporarily, to Brooklands, so comprehensive was the array of parts laid out. Peter Burt himself told *The Auto* reporter that the tool depot alone was enough to frighten and deter any car from stopping.

The car differed to some extent from standard. The rear axle ratio was raised to 3.25 to 1 and the compression ratio may have been changed: indeed the late George Cutbush told the writer that it had been, and quoted a figure of 5.22 to 1, which gave an output of 55bhp at 2800 rpm against the normal 32bhp at 2000 rpm. There was extensive lightening of parts wherever possible. Perrot indicated when the engine needed oil by waving a white flag; as soon as blue smoke appeared from the exhaust he signalled to the driver to stop pumping (there was an extra hand-operated oil pump under his control) by waving a blue flag.

Eight days later, on 27th May, another 14 hour spell began, this time to break world records. In spite of some sparking plug failures and trouble with the petrol-feed line the car ran faultlessly and covered 1,070 miles and 70 yards at an average speed of 76.43 mph, making new world records and new class records. This time one or two members of the Board were in attendance - rather surprisingly, as the general feeling by then was that the directors were singularly uninterested in their company's products.

Argyll badge

In 1914 another records car was prepared, with a 17.3 hp, 2.84 litre engine developing 75 bhp at 3,300 rpm. It had forced lubrication of its sleeve actuating gears, gearshaft bearings, crank journals and big-ends. The worm-drive was replaced by a bevel, for experimental purposes, while there was no differential. Because of the Company's financial problems it did not go to Brooklands, however.

In 1911 a tuned 15/30 was available, with a claimed maximum of 64 mph and towards the end of 1913 a 15/30, with a specially efficient engine, in a sporting-type two seater, was said to be capable of 70 mph. It would be interesting to know something of the 14 hp single sleeve listed in the 1915 *Autocar Buyers' Guide*.

For 1912 the front axle of the 25/50 was located by long radius rods, secured at their rear ends by ball joints, and the springs were free to move at either end. This was dropped from 1913 onwards and was never a feature of the 15/30, but in the 1914 catalogue each model is still shown with radius rods. Differences between the two catalogues in fact are very difficult to spot. The Argyll four-wheel brakes were applied together, either by foot or by hand, and compensation was arranged diagonally. It was a very good design and one that had a long life because of its general soundness and freedom from trouble, elimination of side-slip and lack of effort on the steering. Arrol-Johnston, as we have seen, began earlier with four-wheel brakes (as did Crossley) but gave them up very quickly, claiming that many of their customers distrusted them.

Argyll made most of their own bodywork, at Hozier Street and then at Alexandria. Tales that it was made at a loss may well be true. Certainly it was made to high standards and comprehensively equipped with good weather protection in closed cars. The Streamline Torpedo anticipated the shape of post-war touring cars as early as 1912 and even had something in common with the 12/40 Fast Tourer of 1925. The pre-war landaulette was specially designed for the use of ladies, its opening head being so designed that the owner could operate it from her position of isolated state in the spacious rear compartment without requiring the 'intrusion of her male driver'. The external appearance had much in common with the fashions worn by the prosperous middle-aged or elderly females who favoured it during the few years before the outbreak of war in 1914.

At the acrimonious meeting of shareholders in June 1914 two opposite points of view were presented. The Chairman of Argyll Limited, R W Blackwell, said that the company should have devoted all its energies and capital to the production of a standard car and not wasted its substance (in effect) on a plunge into the unknown. The single sleeve engine had been developed from paper at the company's expense and litigation followed as might have been expected. He asked why such a departure had been made at a time when the company was so short of funds.

At the same meeting John Matthew made a statement that was given less attention than it might, or ought to, have been: he drew the meeting's attention to the fact that the present deficit was a modest sum compared to the £360,000 of 1908, and required nothing like the statesmanship of that time to resolve it. Although Matthew had his supporters at the time, they were outnumbered by the anti-sleeve-valve brigade, and it was resolved to wind up the company. Sir John McLeod CA and Robert Smith CA were appointed joint liquidators. In December 1914, they announced that the works, plant and land had been bought by the Admiralty for £153,000; and during the war, under the control of Sir W G Armstrong-Whitworth, munitions were produced on an extensive scale.

Arrol-Johnston badge

I have already referred to the fact that many, if not all, of the Board members were not particularly interested in the company and did little or nothing to support it when times became difficult. This was certainly not the case so far as the staff was concerned, their loyalty to their managing director being notably close and faithful. Of the feelings of the workmen in general nothing positive can be said; their side of things was seldom aired publicly and the only thing we have to go on is Alex Govan's recorded comments about his workforce in that *Glasgow Herald* obituary. That did indicate some difference of opinion between management and labour - in these days not unexpected, after all. The loss of upwards of 1,500 jobs in 1908, in an area of low employment, must have been hard to bear, not to speak of the wider implications for related industries. The fact that employment was found when the works was turned over to the manufacture of munitions was a temporary measure only and, after the armistice (apart from a short break during the '20s when the plant became a silk mill) there was no further employment until the onset of the Second World War.

I knew, and greatly respected, A K Stevenson, the Secretary of the Royal Scottish Automobile Club during the '50s and before; a man very close to the Scottish industry in its heyday. After he retired I discovered that he had assisted R J Smith, the liquidator of the second Argyll company, in 1914. I rushed into town to ask him what really happened. I suppose his answer is what, knowing his character, I might have expected.

> *I'm not going to tell you, George, because some of the people involved are still alive and I don't want to hurt anyone's feelings*

That old-fashioned, gentlemanly attitude I respected, but it left me with a question that remains unanswered.

Let us now take a look at the rest of the Scottish motor industry, its successes and its failures. There were, in fact, more than 30 makes prior to the Second World War, one of which lost a great deal of money in little more than a year and led to the bankruptcy of George Johnston. On the other hand the establishment of the Scottish Motor Traction Company in 1905 showed what Scotland could do when she chose to go about matters in a thoroughly professional way.

The fact that this was not the case with so much of the industry had a lot to do with its lack of commercial success. The Madelvic was the first make to go into liquidation. By all accounts William Peck was an able astronomer who did much to interest the youth of Edinburgh in his observatory and he was not short of ideas when it came to the motor vehicle. The trouble with his ideas, however, was that so few were of any real practical value.

John Stirling was an extremely keen and energetic automobilist who did a great deal to popularise motoring in his early years. His well-publicised long-distance runs in the late '90s helped to accustom people to the idea of travelling reasonable distances by car. Nothing was ever said about mechanical or other problems on these trips, however. Along with some other manufacturers, Stirling took the sensible way out as far as design and construction were concerned, buying-in his chassis and running gear and adding bodies of his own construction. That worked for a while: he began to advertise launches and then buses. He moved his works to Granton, to the former Madelvic, then Kingsburgh, works and there concentrated largely on buses. The move to Granton took place towards the end of 1903; by August 1904 John Stirling had resigned, and confirmation of the liquidation took place on 24th February 1905. Things did not go well for Stirling thereafter.

The first change of ownership of the Madelvic Motor Carriage Works had taken place in 1900 with the formation of the Kingsburgh Motor Construction Co Ltd, on 18th October. The works, which had cost Peck £33,000 to build and equip, was sold to Kingsburgh for £13,000, the vendor (a director who, incidentally, remained a director of the new company) clearing almost £2,000 on the deal. Although the nominal capital of Kingsburgh was £50,000 in £10 shares, and each subscriber had to have a holding of 500, by 1904 only 4,270 had been received and no more than a handful of vehicles had been built.

In November 1905 the Scottish Motor Engineering Co Ltd was registered. The Naismiths, a family of printers and publishers in Hamilton, who had largely financed Stirling's Motor Construction Co (1903) Ltd, with capital of £120,000 (but only £657 had been called and received by December 1904) sold out to the Scottish Motor Engineering Co Ltd, which was registered on 3rd November 1905, with a more modest capital (on paper at least) of £40,000 in £1 shares. There was no payment for goodwill. The purchase price was £17,500 - £10,000 in cash and £7,500 in £1 shares.

The managing director, John Clingoe, who had had a previous connection with S F Edge, was retained at a salary of £1,000 a year. The Naismiths lost heavily. The works made a few Granton lorries and buses but went into liquidation in January 1907.

As far as I can make out the next occupant of Granton was the Caledonian Motor Engineering Co Ltd which, in 1910, was making a 16 hp Caledonian taxi-cab. In December 1909 it announced an order for 200 cabs, the first of which were due to appear in London that week. Special Muir shock-shifting hubs were fitted, along with Sankey steel wheels, a combination reckoned to reduce tyre bills. Whether it did or not we shall never know... On 30th March 1910, William Peck (and others) took over the assets of the Caledonian Company. Its capital was £36,000 - 31,000 preference shares of £1 and 10,000 ordinary shares of one shilling. His intention was to build a taxi-cab, at least one large order, according to him, having been received from London. The company was one of the shortest-lived in the whole of Scottish industrial history, the resolution to wind up being taken on 9th June 1910. In October 1911 the company was dissolved.

There was a very large loss. In report 24, John Stewart Gowans CA Edinburgh, 'In the reporter's opinion this is a case where the liquidator should make a very exhaustive investigation into the whole affairs of the Company, and submit to the creditors and shareholders a report as to how the very large losses were incurred.'

How Peck financed the purchase of the Caledonian Company is scarcely clear from surviving records. He had received a certain amount of money from William Beardmore & Co for patent rights to a marine oil engine, for the production of which a special plant was to be laid down. Peck's intention was to manufacture commercial vehicles and taxi-cabs, the latter to be fitted with a 16 hp, four-cylinder engine of 3- x 4 bore and stroke respectively. According to his sederunt book

> *... he built the works for Mr Cox and that company (Madelvic) went into liquidation at Mr Cox's death. I purchased these works for £3,500 from the liquidator... which included the whole property, heritable and moveable, fixtures, plant and machinery, with some money of my own and some that I got the use of. I had £2,000 when I took over the works at Granton. I got a bond of £8,000.*
>
> *I took over the works principally for the purpose of carrying on the manufacture of commercial motor vehicles and also to design a special taxi-cab which I called PECK'S taxi-cab. Development cost about £19,000.*

Effectively that was the end of Peck's connection with the Scottish motor industry. A correspondent of mine, Mr Gumley, remembers seeing him round about the end of the First World War, polishing the radiator of his Napier outside his Edinburgh house. By then he had been knighted. He died in 1924.

The failure of the All British Car Company in 1907 was also the end of George Johnston's career in the Scottish motor industry. He was declared bankrupt in 1908 with no assets and liabilities of £16,386. Yet, when he first appeared in court under threat of arrest, on 2nd April 1908, his Bank Statement showed a credit balance of £43,875.

Werbell car, c1908

Eventually, Johnston was cleared completely.

> *The Bankrupt has made a fair discovery and surrender of his Estate and has not been guilty of any collusion, but that his bankruptcy has arisen from innocent misfortune and not from culpable or undue misfortune. The failure of All British Car Co, in turn caused by failure of Contractor to implement his arrangement.*

Some time after he left Arrol-Johnston, George Johnston set up his own company to make cars and commercial vehicles and buses and it was this concern that the All British Car Co Ltd took over in March 1906. At that time the factory had recently been established and was well equipped with the latest machine tools, and Messrs Johnston and Co had undertaken to raise the capacity of their works to 15 cars a week, as part of the selling arrangement.

Technically their engines were of great interest; it was clear that Johnston had lost none of his inventive powers, the 54 hp vertical eight-cylinder unit being useable as a two, four, six or eight according to need. Its cylinders were arranged in two parallel lines of four and sliding camshafts were used to control the numbers of cylinders in use.

The bus chassis was a double-decker, with a horizontal under-floor engine set across the frame, with its cylinders facing forwards. Exceptionally long connecting rods were universally jointed at their big-ends. A chain carried the drive back to a countershaft that carried three chain drives to a differential countershaft from which side chains drove the rear wheels. These were all silent chains and dog-clutches engaged the required gear. As *Motor World* said in May 1907

> *In view of the present situation as regards the merits or demerits of the existing types of London motor omnibuses, the behaviour of the interestingly-designed All-British omnibus when placed on the road will be awaited with considerable interest.*

It is a great pity that no one seems to have made any record of the outcome.

For once *Motor World* went out of its way to lambast the company; the sub-heading of its attack being 'Inefficient Management'. This was amply supported by facts and figures. The company was bought for £74,000 - £44,500 in cash and £30,000 in shares; but the value of stock and materials at the inception of the company was only £8,260. Johnston & Co agreed to hand over the business free of liabilities, with all the plant, machinery and fittings required for a guaranteed output of 15 chassis per week - according to *Motor World* a clumsy arrangement. The 'astounding charge of £15,000 was made for goodwill' - and for patents, too, neither figure being justifiable in the event.

The trading loss between 1st January 1906 and 5th December 1907 was £33,688 and in total (taking into account the £30,000) the overall loss was £119,847. The liquidator stated that a portion of the unpaid calls owing to the vendors or their nominees had been assigned to the directors who guaranteed the bank overdraft - at the date of liquidation standing at £28,511. 'The directors appeared to have suffered grievously, but on the other hand, they are reprehensible for failing to guard the interests of their shareholders.'

Argyll and Arrol-Johnston were to last for the best part of 30 years more and Albion even longer, under Scottish control, until 1951. Not one of the others - and my total is around 80 in all - lasted anything like as long. In what follows I give the approximate life of each company in turn. The Bell dogcart - a creation of Laurence Bell of Peebles - was a one-off, and may have been in existence in 1900 or even earlier: it has been reported to me that a Bell steam-car was built and survived in the Art Gallery and Museum, Kelvingrove, until after the Second World War. The Caledonian began very limited production in Aberdeen in the late '90s and lasted until 1906 or thereabouts. The Cassel (or Chassel) of Glasgow lasted from 1900 to 1903 and I, for one, would like to know something more about it than I do! The Harper and the Mowat (both from Aberdeen, incidentally) were turn-of-the-century productions. The Harper was in small-scale production into the 20th century whereas the Mowat was made for a foreman of that company who had been active in automobile work in the city towards the end of the last century. The Kingsburgh has already been dealt with (it lasted until 1903 or so but it is doubtful if more than one or two prototypes were made), the Robertson (of Dundee) lasted from 1900 until 1903 (and again, little is known about it), the Simpson began to take itself seriously in 1900, lasted certainly until 1904, and John Simpson, engineer, was a director of Grampian Engineering and Motor Company when it was founded in Stirling, in 1907. The St Vincent, from Glasgow, lasted until 1910 in bus, car and taxi form. Walter Bergius's Kelvin car had a three-year life, from 1904 until 1907, and although it was not a success the marine engines that it spawned certainly were, so that the company survives to this day.

In 1906 the Sentinel steam-lorry made it first appearance and, from its very beginning, was a success. So much so, in fact, that the whole operation was moved south, in 1915, to be closer to its main market. The Sentinel and the Albion were equally well known for reliability.

In 1905 the Scotia from Glasgow, came on the market - and was gone again within a year; but the Bon Car from Leith, in steam car form, lasted until 1907. The Drummond, later the North British, was the first car to come out of Dumfries, in 1905, built for the RSAC Reliability Trials by D McKay Drummond of the Dumfries Brass and Iron Foundry Co. The Foundry was taken over for £3,500 and there were four Drummonds on the board along with four other directors. In 1906 the company changed its name to the North British Motor Manufacturing Co Ltd and made a few cars until 1908. Liquidation was agreed in February 1908/1909. The 16-20 Drummond looked very much like the 12/14 Argyll of the previous year.

Five different makes emerged in 1906 but only the Morton lasted for any time. The parent company had been founded in the late 1850s and had produced the occasional steam or electric vehicle from 1897 onwards. The business of R Morton & Son Ltd was taken over by Belhaven Engineering and Motors Ltd on 4th May 1907 and the production of petrol lorries, buses and cars began and was to continue until 1924, with a change of management fairly early on. The purchase price was £62,000. The original directors were dismissed in 1911 and their places taken by David Maxwell and Thomas Elliot, in 1912. A taxi-cab with an Aster engine was in production in 1908. It was built at the Allanton Foundry in Wishaw.

Of the Granton, mention has already been made. The Victoria was built in small quantities in Glasgow in 1906 and 1907 and from Paisley, also in the mid Edwardian era, came the Seetstu (its name possibly intended as a pun, since Seestu was an ancient name for the town) a two-seater vehicle in tricar form by James McGeoch. At the same time Anderston-Grice of Carnoustie introduced the Dalhousie, which was designed by A G Grice, later of GWK, and was notable for its steeply raked radiator. In 1910 James Law of Arbroath bought all the remaining bits but it seems unlikely that he did anything with them. To some extent this car anticipated the look of the latter-day Volvo, with that steeply sloping radiator.

The Dalgleish-Gullane made in Gullane in 1907 was an improved De Dion of much earlier date, and one example survives, a relic of the former

A Kelvin car of 1906, as produced by the Bergius Car and Engine Co, 169 Finnieston Street, Glasgow

motor museum at Clermiston, in Edinburgh. I remember it as a strangely archaic-looking little vehicle. Two entrants in the 1907 RSAC Reliability Trials were 20/24 Werbells from Dundee, produced by Edward and William Raikes Bell. One was 11th in class 4 and the other 8th in class 5.

Another reasonably successful entrant in those Trials was a St Vincent, which was second in class 6 while a car of earlier origin, an Ailsa 15/20, came 6th in class 2. Both came from Glasgow. Hugh Kennedy had actually founded the Kennedy Motor Co Ltd in February 1904, with himself as a director along with William Weir (later Lord Weir), John R (later Sir John) Richmond and the Marquis of Ailsa. Weir, incidentally, had experimented with a car chassis before that time but had decided not to enter motor manufacture. He and Richmond had resigned by February 1907 and their places were taken by Robert Kennedy Snr and

James Kennedy. There were, in time, many more changes of directorate, and by the end of 1907 the entire capital had been taken up with no further issue until after the First World War. In 1917 Kennedy's (Carntyne) Ltd was established at Koh-I-Noor Valve Works, Carntyne, with a capital of £1,000, in £1 shares. By then there were only two directors; Robert Kennedy, who had 997 shares, Hugh Kennedy, who had two, and Robert Kennedy Jnr, who had one.

During 1908 the Alex, the Atholl and the Grampian appeared. Henry Alexander of Alexander and Company in Edinburgh, it is said, designed an engine and possibly a chassis as well. The Atholl was made at Cardonald in Glasgow and was available in car and commercial forms. Again, however, it did not survive for very long. The Grampian was made, in very small numbers, by the Grampian Engineering Company of Stirling during its brief life.

Between 1909 and 1911, approximately, the Cotton car was made in Glasgow. It had been specially designed to cope with the Australian outback, having a 20-24 hp White and Poppe engine with a power take-off so that it could pull itself out of trouble if necessary. It was mounted on outsize wheels with 920x120mm Spencer-Moulton tyrès. Ground clearance was 15 in. Its designer was A J Cotton and it was manufactured by Rennie and Prosser, all examples being exported. (One remains today in New South Wales and is being restored.)

Douglas Fraser and Sons of Arbroath made a few three-and-four-cylinder steam cars in 1911 but did not attempt to carry on production although one member of the family retained his interest in steam traction until well after the Second World War. In 1914 the amphibious Lambert carried out some experiments in Loch Lomond, where its unconventional appearance attracted much attention. It was, as a matter of fact, something of a lash-up, but it had been well thought out and was as mobile on water as it was on land. A single cylinder, $4^1/2$ hp, water-cooled engine drove the rear wheels by a single chain, and afloat a small propellor was driven by an extra bevel, engaged by a dog clutch. On land it could manage about 16 mph; afloat 4 mph.

At the outbreak of war the Scottish motor vehicle industry had shrunk very considerably with an output of around 1,000 vehicles in all, half of which were commercials or buses. At the end of 1914 Albion's paid-up capital amounted to £211,953 and its output totalled 591 chassis and 95 engines. It now held a leading position in the industry at home and overseas that it was to retain for the best part of forty years.

Of the car manufacturers only Arrol-Johnston was still a force to be reckoned with, production being around 500 in the last year of peace: but that was its swansong.

Albion badge

Chapter Three

The End of the Road
1918 to the present day

J. B. Skeoch driving one of his light cars, 1921

After the Armistice it seemed certain that the Scottish Motor Industry was going to share in the general prosperity then enjoyed by the British Isles. Many of those Scots fortunate to return from the battlefields of the world unharmed had money to spare, a taste for the self-propelled vehicle in one or other of its forms and by 1921 their demand was largely satisfied - sooner, in fact, than most people thought.

In 1920 the returning Scot was somewhat restricted in his choice. There was nothing small and cheap and Scottish then - and when a proper Utility, the Skeoch, appeared in 1921 its life was brief, the Dalbeattie works and its contents being consumed by fire in December, soon after their opening. There was nothing to compare with the Rover 8 or, from 1923 onwards, the Austin 7, and nothing comparable in terms of value for money with the Bullnose Morris, the Clyno or the Austin 12, for example.

I deliberately choose to use the word worthy in describing the post-war Scottish cars, for that is what they were, on the whole. They were aimed at the middle class market and were priced accordingly, as long as it was necessary. In 1920 the revived 15.9 hp Argyll tourer was £900 but by 1924, however, its cost had been reduced to £725. The 15.9 hp Arrol-Johnston was £625 in 1920 and by 1928 it was down to £385, at which time the cost of a Morris Oxford tourer was £315. The price difference can be explained by the very much greater output of the English company especially by then, when the number of Arrol-Johnston cars being made was almost nil. Low output had a great deal to do with the higher prices of Scottish cars.

Scotland had nothing to compare with the Model T Ford which, by 1928 was selling in tourer form at £150. In many ways it was the ideal car for

Scottish conditions and sales figures reflected this fact. The flat-nose Morris Cowley of 1928 was £10 more, at £160, which was very competitive, whereas the Austin 12 was £255, which was not. But it was well liked by the Scottish farmer of the more prosperous sort.

The Model T Ford was non pareil, of course; few cars in motoring history have matched it for its combination of toughness and simplicity, for ease of driving and ease of repair and for all-round economy in every sense. There was certainly nothing to compare with it, either from Scotland or from England, for that matter.

Arrol-Johnston came out of the war in the strongest position among the few makes of car left and had modestly ambitious plans for the manufacture of three different makes of car, two of which were to be altogether new. The Beardmore was planned on the grandest scale, with private cars from former munitions factories in Anniesland, and Coatbridge and a taxi-cab from Underwood in Paisley. The latter was built in large numbers and was certainly the best vehicle of its kind to come out of Scotland. Its design had been most carefully considered and developed since the day in 1915 when the decision had been made to build it after the war.

To begin with Arrol-Johnston pinned their hopes on a new Victory model, the designer of which, W A Brown, relied greatly on his wartime aeronautical experience, especially in weight reduction. In the Company's advertising in 1919 it was claimed that 'the Victory model is being built for reputation rather than for profit. A state of affairs which merits the keen attention of every Scot.' The latter had been well aware of its existence since the previous year, when there had been a minor barrage of press notices and comments on a wide scale. Features of the overhead-valve engine included detachable head and liners, CAV dynamo and starter motor and Zenith carburettor (all integral with the engine) and a British magneto. Throughout the maximum use of aeronautical materials was made for the saving of weight.

Victory model, Arrol-Johnston 1919

The gearbox had four speeds and reverse and ran in oil, the loss of power through operation of the gears being less than 6%, it was claimed. The rear axle casing and cover tube were made of aero-engine aluminium and could be lifted by one man yet had a 'hitherto unknown factor of safety.'

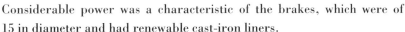

The ill-fated Arrol-Johnston Victory model, as supplied to HRH The Prince of Wales

Considerable power was a characteristic of the brakes, which were of 15 in diameter and had renewable cast-iron liners.

The chassis weighed only 13 cwt unladen. It was as well that the normal 15.9 was still in production because the first private owner of the Victory, H R H The Prince of Wales, was so dissatisfied with his car that he returned it from a tour to the works forthwith, wanting no more to do with it. Production of this very short-lived tourer was stopped at once and the name withdrawn immediately from advertising. The other 15.9, little changed from pre-war cars apart from its radiator which was now of conventional pattern, took its place, selling in modest numbers until 1928 or so.

After Pullinger had been round the world in 1923 there were minor changes in name and small increases in power, the Empire and Dominion eventually emerging to have a go at the export market, with slightly more powerful engines (latterly of the overhead-valve type). In this they were neither more nor less successful than rivals in the same limited field at that time. The widespread North American monopoly of the world's export industry was not to be challenged so easily.

In 1917 the Argyll Company had been revived by J D Brimlow along with three other directors - John Anderson, builder; John Ferguson, civil engineer; R J E Harrison, engineer - optimists to a man, it must be said. The declared capital was £50,000, in £1 shares, and according to the original record Brimlow had 15,000, Anderson 15,000, Ferguson 7,500 and Harrison 7,500. There were numerous changes of director in subsequent years. On 12th January 1923 the overdraft was £25,000 - the limit, then, perhaps? - and the amount overdrawn was £15,106 6s 9d. Thereafter it fluctuated; by 31 December 1928 it stood at £36,773 14s 5d, and by 1 April 1932 it was £40,022 8s 11d. In 1934 the Company went into voluntary liquidation. In 1960 there was still a credit balance of £3,867 19s 4d, because of an unsettled dispute and the final winding-up had never been completed because of this.

Two directors of Argyll at different times were John Anderson, almost certainly a principal of P & W Anderson, the builders of the office block at Alexandria, and John Ferguson, a principal of Ferguson, Allan & Co, who were contractors for the works at Alexandria. Such long-term loyalty to the Company was, perhaps, somewhat unusual.

The revived 15/30 Argyll had a production life of about five years and possibly a dozen chassis were made in all. Engine supplies seem to have been a problem. The post-war car featured disc wheels, along with spiral bevel final drive, unit construction of gearbox and engine, and cantilever rear suspension. The price of the tourer pre-war had been £575.

A smaller chassis was introduced in 1922, a four-cylinder rated at 11.4 hp, with a capacity of 1,496 cc and an output of 30 bhp, at 3,000 rpm. Four-wheel brakes were fitted in 1928, which was really the last year of serious production. From 1925 a sporting version was available, with a 1,630 cc engine, rated at 12.5 hp and developing no less than 42 bhp at 3,200 rpm. It still looked like a touring car, however, a matter of simple economics, no doubt, but a marketing error of a kind that someone as intelligent as Cecil Kimber of MG would never have made; nor would Argyll under the direction of Alex Govan or John Matthew.

I have a report from someone who occupied premises next door to John Brimlow at the beginning of the '30s. He sat, bowler-hatted, throughout the day, surrounded by petrol tanks, steering wheels on their columns and many more spares and was accompanied by a bust of either Govan or himself. Apparently he was an agreeable neighbour.

A 1922 Arrol-Johnston All Weather tourer with body by Penman of Dumfries, delivered to the Isle of Wight, March 1922, registration number DL2560. This vehicle was sold in the Sword Sale in March 1965 and in the 1990s is still in running order. (Photo George Oliver archive, Museum of Transport)

In 1920 Carlaw, who were well known as makers of ticket-printing machines in Glasgow and had dabbled with car design in the early 1900s making a prototype two-cylinder, 8 hp engine, entered the goods vehicle market with a 1 ton chassis built on American lines, which they promptly sold within a couple of months of exhibiting it at the Scottish Show to the Harper-Bean concern in Manchester (which may have been involved in the work on prototypes), for a good deal more than the whole project had cost them, and as George Cutbush wrote a long time afterwards -

...few who have built cars or commercials in Scotland have ever achieved that much.

The Milton, from Edinburgh, which had its origins with William Foulis Ltd, a company established to deal in cars, especially those made by Porthos, a year or two before the First World War (and with the sole right to sell them in Scotland) was made during 1921 and was a water-cooled four-cylinder. It had a Decolange engine of 10.5 hp, and final drive was by friction - the only example of its kind in Scotland as far as I know. It was available in two- and four-seat forms but its life was brief.

In 1921 the Gilchrist appeared from Govan, with an overhead-valve engine supplied by Hotchkiss of Coventry, a concern very much better known for their side-valve engines for the Bullnose Morris. To begin with the chassis price was £475 and the tourer sold at £625. By the end of 1922, however, the latter had been reduced to £475. Production stopped in 1923 and although the Gilchrist did not sell in large numbers it appears to have satisfied those who bought it.

During 1921 the Skeoch was made for a short time. It was the only Scottish cyclecar, with a single-cylinder, air-cooled two-stroke of 348 cc, driving the solid rear axle through a two-speed gearbox, but as we have learned a fire in December 1921 destroyed the works and all that they contained. The Skeoch was of quite distinctive appearance and sold at £165 or £180 according to specification. Production was not resumed because the factory and its contents had been uninsured.

Beardmore Mark 1 taxi, 1920 produced by the Bergius Car and Engine Co

Right above
Skeoch Utility Car, 1921

Right below
A view of the Skeoch works, Burnside, Dalbeattie, 1921

SKEOCH UTILITY CAR

Manufactured by

THE SKEOCH UTILITY CAR CO.

Dalbeattie, Scotland.

The Reliable and Economical Small Car at last.

PRICE COMPLETE - £180

LESS ACCESSORIES, £165

In 1922 the Scotsman light car of 10 hp was built in Glasgow. Three models were marketed - a Utility 11 hp, a 10-20 Standard and a 14-40. The Utility had side valves, a four-speed gearbox - unusual at that time in a car of such low power - steel disc wheels and a top speed according to The Light Car, which tested an early production model in 1922, of about 45 mph. The four-seat Utility cost £425 complete, the 10-12 All-Weather Standard £495 and the 14-40 five-seat de luxe £550. Not too much was made of the fact that Sir Harry Lauder was a director, along with John Hall Nicol. The Company was in liquidation by 1924.

Another patriotically-named car, the Rob Roy, also appeared from Glasgow in 1922. It had a Koh-I-Noor 8 hp, twin horizontally-opposed engine, made by the Kennedy Motor Co at Carntyne. It was a good-looking car, costing £285 and there was a de luxe version at £325. Later a sports version was on offer at £190 and a new Dorman-engined four-cylinder soon joined it. In 1924 the flat-twin was continued, along with a 10-12 and 12-20. They were not successful, however; the market for twins was fast disappearing and the four-cylinder cars had little appeal.

At the 1922 Scottish Show seven Rob Roys were on show altogether, including complete cars finshed in Ivory White, Mole Puttee and Koh-I-Noor Red, a coupé by John Boyd of Glasgow and a polished chassis.

Rob Roy car built by Hugh Kennedy, 1922

Miss Dorothée Pullinger

The Scotsman, in two forms, was almost the last of the Scottish cars. In its original Edinburgh form it had a six-cylinder, air-cooled engine of French manufacture, the SARA. This unit had had some racing successes in France over a number of years. In February 1930 it was replaced by the Little Scotsman, which had a water cooled four-cylinder 11.9 hp engine of 1,497 cc and 12/40 rated power. Scotsman Motors Ltd was short-lived; it was incorporated on 11th November 1928 and in liquidation by 9th May 1930. Final liabilities were £7,472 17s 3d against assets of £1,006 9s 11d. At a sale of finished cars on 13th June 1930 prices of £160, £165 and £167 10s were realised.

In February 1930 the Little Scotsman Royal Scot two-seater was listed at £435 (£555 in supercharged form), the Gleneagles sportsman's coupé at £445 (£565 supercharged) and the Braemar saloon at £455. These were not particularly low prices at that time and the market was much too limited for commercial success, especially then, when Britain was entering a state of economic depression.

Richard Henry Birkin, a lace manufacturer of Nottingham, had 500 shares in Scotsman Motors and one wonders if he was related to Sir Henry Birkin, the well-known driver of Bentleys at that time.

The Galloway began as a private venture by Pullinger, in a wartime works at Tongland, near Kirkcudbright, on the banks of the River Dee.

Although this building was not completed until after the war was over aero-engine manufacture was carried out on a quite extensive scale there and a high percentage of the workforce was female. Dorothée Pullinger, one of Pullinger's numerous children, was a director of Galloway and did a certain amount of competition driving, with some success.

Little change was made to the Galloway during a production life that began in 1921 and lasted until round about the closing of Heathhall in 1929. It had a simple four-cylinder engine of 10.5 hp for the first two years, after which it was uprated to 10.9 hp. It was designed specifically for doctors and other professional persons and the cost, at the beginning, was £550. A two-seat coupé was first available, then a four-seater and finally a saloon. The Galloway was a sturdy car resembling in performance the Fiat 501 from which its design had been drawn.

When the Beardmore Company was established in 1919 it took over the Aidee Motor and Engineering Company Limited of Motherwell who were

*A Heathhall-built Galloway
at the Dumfries works*

*The Galloway Engineering
works, Tongland*

Tongland-built 10.5hp Galloway light car, 1921

makers of and dealers in motor cars, carriages, vehicles and boats, aero-engines, aeroplanes, motor launches, etc. Its stated capital was £100,000, in shares, and the directors were Sir William Beardmore Bart, J G Girdwood, F M Luther and G H Allsworth, the latter being nominees of Aidee Limited. Luther had been known before the war for his connection with the Austro-Daimler car and the Beardmore Company was known for its association with the Austro-Daimler aero-engine.

The smallest of the new Beardmores was of 11.5 hp, with overhead camshaft operated overhead valves, three speeds and reverse, a plate clutch and spiral bevel final drive. There was a much larger chassis, the 20-30, made at Coatbridge and exhibited at several motor shows before disappearing without trace. The only owner I know of was Lord Reith when, as plain Mr Reith, he was manager of the Speedwell Works at Coatbridge and had a 30 as official car.

In 1911 the 30 hp Beardmore cost more than £1,000, which put it high on British, let alone Scottish, price lists. The third Beardmore (which had the same engine as the taxi, detuned to some slight extent) did not have a

Anderson Special at Killoup Hill, Girvan, 6th March 1936. Premier award winner in over 1500cc class.

long production life. Two of the three were models listed in 1924 were rated as 12.8s and were substantial cars. Three were in the Sword Collection until its dispersal. There was much publicity material about Arrol-Johnston, Beardmore and Galloway products in *The Beardmore News*, a regular publication which dealt also with other forms of transport manufactured by the Group - motor cycles, locomotives, etc, and ships of various kinds. It was all rather serious and I intend not too much disrespect if I liken its contents at times to the duller sort of church magazine.

In 1927 there was an amalgamation between Arrol-Johnston and the Aster Engineering Company of Wembley which, effectively, put four makes of car under one roof.

By then sales were poor and during the next year or so they dwindled away to nothing. In 1929, for example, the costliest Aster was £1,200, which took it close to the price of a Lanchester 21 hp or a large Sunbeam. For 1928 the Arrol-Aster models were a six-cylinder, single-sleeve and a six-cylinder, overhead-valve, rated as 17/50 and 21/60 hp, respectively. The fact that we have always been able to hold our own in world matters suggests that when we want to do something badly enough we will find ways and means to do so.

Perhaps those formerly concerned with the making and marketing of motor cars in Scotland were not fully committed - perhaps the death-wish was there from the beginning, hidden, silent, inevitable. Those who created the industry were, at the same time, securing its eventual destruction. I think that this may have been the fundamental reason for the failure of the Scot to stay in it.

Certainly he was early enough on the motoring scene. Several cars were assembled here during the '90s and manufacturing on a commercial scale was under way shortly after the beginning of the present century. There seemed to be no very obvious reason for thinking that Scottish cars would not have as considerable an international success as ships from Scottish yards, whisky from Scottish distilleries and tweed from Scottish mills. Some did go overseas - notably the three As, Albion, Arrol-Johnston and Argyll. But, Albion apart, these firms failed to establish themselves in potentially valuable markets for which the sturdiness of their products might have made them especially suitable.

What are the Scottish cars that I remember from my childhood? Precious few, alas. There was the local garage man's Argyll landaulet, which spent most of its time at the road-side, *en panne* as the French would say (but we said "Mac's motor's busted again"). I have a hazy recollection of seeing the odd Galloway and there must have been other, more modern, Argylls around. I do remember one or two Arrol-Asters, mainly because they were large and somewhat impressive; at the same time I have an idea that I remember people telling me that they were not particularly reliable.

The last of the series of Anderson Specials built by Anderson of Newton Mearns

No Scottish car aroused my interest or fired my imagination in the way that a Bullnose Morris or M Type MG could do. The skirl of a Bullnose in second gear was one of the accepted sounds of one's childhood; one grew up with it, recognised it from afar, imitated it. Eventually one might change one's allegiance to another make but the chances were that the early interest would be retained and would influence one's buying later on. I cannot think of a single Scottish car that affected me in that way.

It can be said, I know, that the Bullnose Morris cost very much less to buy than a Scottish car of comparable power and size such as the smaller Galloway. The Scottish manufacturer was not really catering for the mass market and here he made one of his basic mistakes. Concentration on quality is all very well but it is important to provide value for money at the same time. Of the Scottish makes only Argyll seemed to me to do that successfully - and the only person who gained any advantage was the customer! Before the First World War Arrol-Johnston were already running their body-shop at a sizeable loss. Cost control may have been heard of but from all accounts it would appear that no one applied it in practice.

We are renowned for our canniness and caution, but surely we let it take over completely where the production of motor-cars was concerned. George Johnston, who really began the Scottish motor industry as such, was one of the canniest of all. Like the German pioneer Benz he saw no particularly strong reason for change and this reluctance to move with the technical times led both men into commercial difficulties for a while. Until mass-production techniques became widely adopted it was relatively easy to change a design in order to take maximum advantage of the latest technical advances. Johnston resisted change, however beneficial it might be, and was still pushing his long out-of-date dogcarts as late as 1901.

The shape of the Arrol-Johnston dogcart was distinctive because it was so archaic: like its performance it had too much to do with the horse-drawn vehicles that had preceded it. In the early 1900s keeping up with the Joneses was every bit as important as it is today. Few motorists cared to be seen perched high above the ground on a machine that had such obvious 19th century connections and was so slow that it could not - literally speaking - keep up with its contemporaries, let alone the Joneses.

The admitted reliability of the dogcart was no longer a sufficiently strong selling factor and, in spite of its popularity with doctors, other cars were proving to be at least as suitable for their specialized needs. There was, for example, no Scottish equivalent of the lively, economical and extremely reliable De Dion single-cylinder. The Argyll voiturette did not stand any real chance against such strong competition.

Yet in many ways the Argyll was the best of the Scottish cars. It was so much the product of an individual that when Alex Govan, its creator, died in 1907 the real life went out of the company.

In the later history of the Alexandria firm we read of nothing but financial difficulties. Most, if not all, had their origins even before Alex Govan died; far too high a proportion was squandered on the building of a sandstone fantasy that was opened in the summer of 1906 so that there was insufficient working capital left. Even earlier, at the very end of the 19th century, Peck, founded the Madelvic Motor Company Ltd. with a capital sum of £21,000. By some financial dexterity that I do not profess to understand he managed to build a factory at Granton at a cost of something like £33,000! But Peck, it appears, was a master salesman.

A Halley lorry built for the Calgary Car Company Ltd – produced in Yoker c1908

He must have been, because after the collapse of his Madelvic Company he reappeared on the Scottish motoring scene with the patriotically named Caledonian Engineering Co, intending to build taxi-cabs. That business also went into liquidation.

They came and they went throughout the 1900s – St Vincent, Werbell, Scottish Aster, St Laurence, Kelvin, Drummond, ABC (George Johnston was connected with this make which had a brief life and helped to involved its sponsors in a loss of £120,000), Atholl Kennedy and Stirling among them. Only Albion, Argyll and Arrol-Johnston showed any signs of permanence - but the first-named company turned all its energies to the production of commercial vehicles from 1913 onwards, and the second went into its final liquidation in the summer of 1914. The turn of the third was yet to come; in the meantime it was in a reasonably healthy state, its well-being greatly helped by the efforts of an imaginative publicity man, Arrol-Johnston advertisements of the period just before the First War are well worth looking at - what a pity that they featured such generally dull motor-cars.

A 1930 Halley lorry as delivered to the George Younger brewery in Alloa

By now the main Arrol-Johnston design inspiration was the Renault - and a better model to copy could not have been easier found. All the same where was Scottish inventiveness?

Argyll were much more adventurous: very early in the field with the use of the word streamlined to describe their smoothly-contoured touring bodies, introducing four-wheel braking (along with Arrol-Johnston) in 1911 they also followed up their adoption of the Burt McCollum sleeve-valve engine by fighting a successful but extremely costly lawsuit with the holders of the Knight sleeve-valve patents. But whatever this gallant company did something went wrong and it is the only one whose failure I genuinely lament. Again, the people concerned had much to do with the company's inability to keep solvent; tales are told of directors who had larger holdings in other car firms, and as a result were less eager to promote Argyll interests. Only Albion seemed to have commercial acumen as well as a really good product and, until the present time, only Albion have continued in business without a break as manufacturers of motor-vehicles North of Hadrian's Wall.

All gone by 1930 or '31 - no one is absolutely certain when the last Scottish car was made although it is not all that long ago, historically speaking. The industry that began in the reign of Queen Victoria ended in the reign of her grandson, George V, almost unnoticed because of the slump that was attracting so much attention everywhere. Was it such a loss to the British motor industry as a whole; was it such a blow to the Scottish economy as all that?

My view - which may be unpopular - is that we were probably well-rid of our little motor industry. By the 1920s we had said all we were able to say about motor-car design; we had nothing new to offer, no light car of universal appeal like the Austin 7, no cheap family man's car with the charm of the Bullnose Morris, no quality car to compare with the Rolls-Royce or Lanchester, no sporting car to compete against the 30/98 Vauxhall or 3 litre Bentley. There were enough dull and really dreary cars being made elsewhere as it was: we didn't even have any advantage there!

I will end by referring once more to my belief that our motor industry was doomed from the beginning as long as its control remained in the hands of Scotsmen. It might have succeeded if it had been a natural thing for the Scot to concern himself with the multiple production of cars. As it was his individualism acted as a hidden brake, prevented him from persevering and did not - as might have been expected, in the circumstances - even encourage him to concentrate on the production of very high-grade, limited production motor-cars. The capital was there (as some of the figures I have quoted may indicate) and there was no real problem just because the best markets were two or three hundred miles south: after all English manufacturers found our country a worthwhile place to sell in and the French and the Americans, who were even further away, found no lack of orders here.

It is now nearly 70 years since Henry Alexander drove a Model T Ford to the top of Ben Nevis. It might have been wise of the Scottish manufacturers then engaged in the motor industry to have sabotaged this revealing demonstration.

Part of the Scottish Built Car Display as seen at Albert Drive 1986. (Photograph George Oliver archive, Museum of Transport)

ARGYLL

Glasgow's Museums of Transport

TURETTE

*One of Glasgow Museums'
Argyll voiturettes before
conservation*

From 1964 to 1987 an expanding and developing Museum of Transport was housed in the former Glasgow Corporation Tramways Works in Albert Drive, Glasgow. In 1964 George Oliver published an article about it in the magazine of the Veteran Car Club. The following are some extracts from this article.

'Variety is an outstanding feature of the recently opened Museum of Transport in Glasgow. The collection of wheeled vehicles is representative of close on 50 years of continuous development and includes horse-drawn types, bicycles, trams, commercials, a bus and a number of cars. The oldest self-propelled vehicle is the chassis of what may well have been one of Sir Goldsworthy Gurney's steam carriages, built in 1828 and operated on a commercial basis between Glasgow and Paisley until 1834 when a rather violent explosion ended its working life. The remains are notable for their sturdiness of construction and simplicity of design.

The newest car on show is the first Hillman Imp to leave the Linwood factory that is within 10 miles of the Museum and the newest vehicle is a Moulton cycle. The latter contrasts strongly with a nearby Hobby Horse of 1819 - a really early example of do-it-yourself transport.

The oldest car in this collection is an 1898 Benz, in a rather uninspiring colour scheme that is hardly typical of the period. It is interesting to compare its appearance with that of an 1898 single-decker tram close by: the latter is much more modern-looking vehicle and might be passed off as vintage rather than veteran. The next oldest cars date from 1900 and perhaps the most interesting is the 1900 Albion A1 chassis, the first

Arrol Aster 17/50 type SV Saloon of 1927 on loan to Glasgow Museum of Transport from the National Museums of Sc

model to be sold. Its enormous horizontally-opposed, twin-cylinder engine occupies about half the length of the chassis and most of its width and looks quite indestructible. No wonder this make established such a high reputation for reliability - the margin of safety must have been enormous.

Two 1900 Argyll voiturettes show clearly the standard of restoration carried out by the Museum Workshop staff. They also show that large-diameter wheels and short wheelbases were a great handicap as far as excellence of appearance was concerned. Along the line there are later models from this maker - a 1907 Aster-engined car that is on loan from the Sword Collection and a 1927 sleeve-valve 12 tourer.

The Arrol-Johnstons are typical of this rather dull make - a completely restored 1901 10 hp dogcart that has none of the majesty of presence that its larger brother had (the extra row of seats makes all the diference as far as this make is concerned) and the 1920 15.9 coupé that was formerly in the Sword Collection. Next to it stands a 1924 Beardmore all-weather that looks typical of its day but conceals an overhead-camshaft engine beneath its bonnet. Other exhibits in this Scottish section are a fine 1910 A3 Albion tourer from its maker's collection and the first truck to be made at the BMC plant at Bathgate.'

Unfortunately no mention by George Oliver of the new Museum of Transport in the Kelvin Hall has been traced. Innovations that would have interested him are: the simulated Glasgow street of 1938, with its period shop fronts and window displays, its street lamps and signs and both private and commercial vehicles parked on its cobbled roadway.

The other principal innovation is the display of mass-produced private cars. These are in the setting of an authentic motor car showroom so that visitors are able to examine the cars closely as if they were potential purchasers. Many have labels giving the original selling price.

In the museum collection of motor cars the emphasis is on the Scottish product and every attempt has been made to acquire and display locally built vehicles when available.

Scottish Cars

MAKE	LOCATION	DATES
ABC	BRIDGETON/GLASGOW	1906-8
AC	HILLINGTON/GLASGOW	1984
ALBION	SCOTSTOUN/GLASGOW	1900-13
ALEX	EDINBURGH	1908
ARGYLL	BRIDGETON/GLASGOW	1899-1906, 1914-32
ARGYLL	LOCHGILPHEAD	1916
ARGYLL	ALEXANDRIA	1906-14
ARROL ASTER	DUMFRIES	1927-31
ARROL JOHNSTON	CAMLACHIE/GLASGOW	1897-1906
ARROL JOHNSTON	PAISLEY	1906-13
ARROL JOHNSTON	DUMFRIES	1913-27
ATHOLL	GLASGOW	1907-8
BEARDMORE	GLASGOW	1920-8
BEARDMORE	PAISLEY	1920-32
BEARDMORE	COATBRIDGE	1920-8
BELHAVEN	WISHAW	1906-24
BON CAR	EDINBURGH	1905-7
CALEDONIAN	ABERDEEN	1899-1906
CALEDONIAN	EDINBURGH	1912-24
CASSELL	GLASGOW	1900-3
CHRYSLER	LINWOOD	1976-9
COTTON	GLASGOW	1911
DALGLEISH- GULLANE	HADDINGTON	1907-8
DALHOUSIE	CARNOUSTIE	1906-10
DLM	MOTHERWELL	1913-20
DRUMMOND	DUMFRIES	1905-9
DUNALISTAIR	GLASGOW	1925-6
FEROX	PAISLEY	1914
FRASER	ARBROATH	1911
GALLOWAY	TONGLAND & DUMFRIES	1921-2, 1923-8

GILCHRIST	GLASGOW	1920-3
HARPER	ABERDEEN	1898-1900, 1905-5
JP	BELLSHILL	1950-4
KELVIN	GLASGOW	1904-6
KENNEDY	GLASGOW	1907-10
KINGSBURGH	EDINBURGH	1901-2
MADELVIC	GRANTON, EDINBURGH	1898-1900
MEARNS	LAURENCEKIRK	1899-1902
MILTON	EDINBURGH	1920-1
NEALE	EDINBURGH	1897
NESIE	EDINBURGH	1897
PROBE	IRVINE	1971
RENFREW	GLASGOW	1904
RIDLEY	PAISLEY	1901-7
ROB ROY	SHETTLESTON/GLASGOW	1922-6
ROBERTSON	DUNDEE	1901-2
ROBERTSON (COWALL)	DRYMEN	1934
ROOTES	LINWOOD	1963-76
ROYAL SCOT	ANNIESLAND/GLASGOW	1922-4
SCAMP	PRESTWICK	1965
SCOTIA	GLASGOW	c1907
SCOTSMAN	GLASGOW	1922-3
SCOTSMAN	EDINBURGH	1929-30
SEETSTU	PAISLEY	1906-7
SIMPSON	MILTON/STIRLING	1897-1904
SKEOCH	DALBEATTIE	1921
STIRLING	HAMILITON & EDINBURGH	1897-1901
ST LAURENCE	LAURENCEKIRK	1899-1902
ST VINCENT	GLASGOW	1903-10
TALBOT	LINWOOD	1979-81
TOD	DUNFERMLINE	1897
WAVERLEY	EDINBURGH	1901-4
WBC	ABERDEEN	1914
WERBELL	DUNDEE	1907-9

Index

Page numbers in bold indicate illustrations

Burt, Peter	52,53,**53**,55,60
Burt, Thomas	55,57
bus, Albion	**13**,16
Caledonian	99
Motor Engineering Co Ltd	64-5,68
Cassel (or Chassel)	10,68,99
Charabanc, Belhaven	**9**
Christian, J P	45,50,51
Chrysler	99
Clark, John F	7
Clingoe, John	64
Commercial	
Albion	**12**,16
Argyll	44,45
Cotton	72,99
'Craigievar Express'	8
Crawford, William	50
Cyclecar	80
DLM	99
Dalgleish-Gullane	70-1,99
Dalhousie	70,99
Darracq Company	52
Davidson, Thomas Dence A	47
Day, Bernard	28
Dei-Donum	3-4
Dogcart	
Albion	viii
Arrol-Johnston	11-12,22,23
Bell	68
Drew & Co, John	6
Drummond	69,99
Dumfries Brass and Iron Foundry Co	69
Dunalistair	99
Electric brougham	4
Elliot, T R B	2
Engineer, The	24
Ferox	99
Ferrier Brown, W	57
Finnieston Street premises	**15**
Fire engine	
Albion Merryweather	**18**
Argyll	49,**49**
Foulis Ltd, William	79
Fraser	99
Fraser and Sons, Douglas	72
Friswell, Chas	36
Fulton, Norman	viii,1,2,11,15
Galloway	83,**84**,**85**,90,99
Engineering Works	**86**
Gilchrist	80,100
Govan, Alex	1-2,33-8,40-1,43-45,62
Grampian	72
Engineering and Motor Company	69,72
Grampian Transport Museum	8
Granton	10,63,64,70
Halley	10
Harper	9,68,100
Heathhall works	31,32
Henderson, J F	15
Hoiland, Edward	55
Hozier Engineering Company	33,**34**,**35**,37,38
Hunter, John	24
Isle of Man Tourist Trophy race	26-9
John O'Groats Journal	24,**24**-5
Johnston, George	1,2,21,24,63,65-7,89
Johnston and Co	66-7,68
Kelvin	69,100
Kennedy	100
Kennedy Motor Co Ltd	71,82
Kennedy's (Carntyne) Ltd	72
Kingsburgh	10,63,68,100
Motor Construction Co Ltd	64
Knight and Kilbourne, Messrs	58
Koh-I-Noor Valve Works	72
Lambert amphibious car	72
Luther, F M	85
McCollum, J H K	53,55
McDonald brothers	5
McGeoch, James	70
Madelvic	100
Carriage Co	8,63,65
electric brougham	4
Matthew, John	47,52,55,57-8,62

HMSO publications are available from:

HMSO Publications Centre
(Mail, fax and telephone orders only)
PO Box 276m London SW8 5DT
Telephone orders 071-873 9090
General enquiries 071-873 0011
(queuing system in operation for both numbers)
Fax orders 071-873 8200

HMSO Bookshops
71 Lothian Road, Edinburgh, EH3 9AZ
031-228 4181 Fax 031-229 2734
49 High Holburn, London, WC1V 6HB
071-873 0011 Fax 071-873 8200 (counter service only)
258 Broad Street, Birmingham, B1 2HE
021-643 3740 Fax 021-643 6510
33 Wine Street, Bristol, BS1 2BQ
0272 264306 Fax 0272 294515
9-12 Princess Street, Manchester, M60 8AS
061-834 7201 Fax 061-833 0634
16 Arthur Street, Belfast, BT1 4GD
0232 238451 Fax 0232 235401

HMSO's Accredited Agents
(see Yellow Pages)

and through good booksellers

Printed in Scotland for HMSO by C.C.Nº 18023 11/93 3OC Dd 287957